New Greek Cuisine

New Greek Cuisine

Aristedes Pasparakis

and

Byron Ayanoglu

HarperCollins*Publishers*Ltd

New Greek Cuisine
© 2005 by Byron Ayanoglu and Aristedes Pasparakis

Published by HarperCollins Publishers Ltd

First edition

HarperCollins books may be purchased for educational,
business, or sales promotional use through our Special
Markets Department.

HarperCollins Publishers Ltd
2 Bloor Street East, 20th Floor
Toronto, Ontario, Canada
M4W 1A8

www.harpercollins.ca

Library and Archives Canada Cataloguing in Publication

Pasparakis, Aristedes, 1942–
New Greek cuisine : fresh and modern recipes from
Aristedes' kitchen / Aristedes Pasparakis and Byron
Ayanoglu. – 1st ed.

ISBN 0-00-639456-6

1. Cookery, Greek. I. Ayanoglu, Byron II. Title.

TX723.5.G8P38 2005   641.59495   C2004-905841-X

Photographs: Hal Roth Photography Inc.
Food styling: Julie Zambonelli
Prop styling: Maggie Jones

RRD 9 8 7 6 5 4 3 2 1

Printed and bound in the United States
Set in Miller

This book is dedicated to the loving memory of my mother,
Christina Pasparakis

Contents

Introduction

The Chef

Aristedes Pasparakis is at the top of the contemporary level of a Greek cookery-pyramid that has its base in pre-history. He epitomizes a culinary exploration that began with the Minoans of Crete some five thousand years ago and that has been evolving over the millennia, always with equal attention paid to health and gustatory pleasure.

This internationally acclaimed chef understands the accomplishments of his ancestors almost as if they were a hereditary trait, establishing him not only as an authority but also as a practitioner who has given diners thirty years' worth of memorable meals. He is one of a select group of chefs who have redefined Greek cuisine and placed it in the same firmament as the other great cuisines of the planet.

But there is nothing immediately hereditary in Aristedes' affinity for the kitchen. He has no personal history of ongoing family restaurants, and he didn't grow up watching his parents and grandparents laboring at the stove. The eldest son of an intellectual, solidly middle-class family with roots in the island of Crete, Aristedes grew up in academic circles in the Anglo-Saxon world (South Africa, England, British Columbia). After he earned a Ph.D. in metallurgical engineering, he taught an interdisciplinary course of his own devising, "Material Science for Artists," to final-year fine arts students at the University of British Columbia.

Legend has it that during a particularly lonely winter evening in his cozy Kitsilano apartment in the early seventies, with the fire dwindling and his latest thesis, half-finished and wrenchingly boring, on his desk, Aristedes had a revelation. Within a week, he had resigned his teaching post, abandoned his research into the stochastic theory of sculpture, and started work on Orestes, a restaurant named after his infant son.

Orestes astonished Vancouver. Here was a Greek restaurant that had no overcooked mystery-meat concoctions languishing at a steam table, no greasy moussakas, no soggy filo pies, no overboiled vegetables, and not a single tooth-challenging cheap-meat-broiled-to-a-crisp posing as souvlaki, the Greek national snack. Instead, at Orestes one feasted on lively seafood, tart and spicy rabbit and onion stew, aromatic combinations of greens and herbs, buttery feta cheese, authentic bean and lentil soups, the lot lovingly perfumed with drizzles of the freshest Cretan olive oil, specially air-freighted to the restaurant. The famously laid-back West Coasters responded with uncharacteristic alacrity, and Orestes took off like a tasty firework.

Aristedes forged that first venue into a Vancouver restaurant empire, with five additional eateries, stretching from North Vancouver to the West End, while in Kitsilano, the original Orestes expanded exponentially into a palace dedicated to Greek-style dining and partying. He toured his domain in a convertible Benz, outfitted in traditional Cretan warrior dress (black shirt, riding pants, knee-high boots, and a kerchief around his long, curly hair).

Vancouver soon grew too small for the larger-than-life chef, and he branched out to Victoria (Al Dente), Calgary (another Orestes), and finally into the major arena of Canadian degustation, Toronto. There he dabbled in a rapid sequence of critically praised, popular eateries, until he settled into the epoch-making Ouzeri, on Danforth Avenue, in the heart of Toronto's Greektown. Here he created a lively, colorful restaurant, with irresistibly perky and refreshing cooking, and an ambience reminiscent of jet-set Mykonos. Instant line-ups formed at Ouzeri's door even before the official opening, and Aristedes' new Greek cuisine, already a staple in his western Canadian establishments, officially arrived on center stage.

The Danforth has never been the same since Ouzeri. No one in their right mind would any longer want to serve old-style Greek food mushy from the steam table or charred to distraction by angry coals. The Aristedes "touch" became the new order of things. He was evolving the method that is at the heart of this cookbook: frying without oil, for a result that is both more healthful and more flavorful. In the Aristedes mold, the oil and many of the flavorings are added at the end of the cooking and so remain full-bodied in the dish.

Aristedes, who had become famous enough to be recognized by his first name all over Canada, by now felt that he had done all he could in the kitchens of this country. He was free to return to Greece and really get to know the homeland. For so many years he had been an ambassador of Greekness, but he had spent hardly any of that time in Greece.

The most remarkable achievement of this remarkable career has been Aristedes' enormous influence in the rethinking of Greek cooking in Greece itself. Since the mid-1990s, Athens has experienced prodigious restaurant activity, as the Greek metropolis has joined, along with every other European capital, the worldwide culinary evolution into the new millennium. Aristedes has been in the spotlight every step of the way. He was one of ten chefs chosen by the Greek Academy of Taste to contribute to a cookbook, published in Paris in seven languages, that has redefined Greek cuisine. He also published a gourmet diet cookbook in Greece and was recognized as the most innovative chef in Greek cuisine for 2000, at a contest held annually in Athens. He was also the chef representing Greece in 2001 at the Symposium of Mediterranean Cooking held in Istanbul.

In the same decade he has been mentor, creative consultant, and, most tellingly, menu designer and educator of the staffs of some thirty new and important restaurants. In the process he has been lionized by the Athenian press and has become synonymous with fine dining in a city that predicates its happiness on eating well.

It takes a special mind, and a particular kind of life, to identify what is at the heart of Greek cuisine, to harness it, and to serve that cuisine in a way that can please, even astound, everyone, be they Greek or not. Aristedes has made it his life's work to do just that. It has taken him thirty years, and dozens of his own restaurants on two continents, but he is now ready to share his best recipes. More than that, Aristedes is ready to reveal his tricks of the trade, cooking techniques that he has perfected over his many years in the kitchen.

The Cuisine

Greek cuisine has its origins in Minoan Crete, an island kingdom from the time of ancient Egypt. Crete, a place drunk with olive oil, developed a cuisine based on that oil and on its plentiful vegetables, legumes, grains, and fish. It was a way of eating that promoted health and longevity and was so toothsome that it has survived the millennia more or less intact, even if the Hellenic world that embraced it has had to endure the vagaries and vicissitudes of a long history.

There are Greeks everywhere on this planet, the result of a restless people who have forever been looking for greener pastures. And wherever there are Greeks, there is Greek cuisine. Reinvented to suit the new environment, be it Asia Minor or Australia, and altered by the passing of time, all Greek cookery is based on the solid principles set out long ago in Crete—though at times, and in particular places, it has stretched the imagination.

The greatest challenge Aristedes has had to contend with is the enormous range of Greek cuisine, the manifold versions of it around the world, and the indiscriminate, sometimes merciless influences that have shaped it over the centuries. He has overcome the confusion by creating his own version of Greek food, incorporating the desirable mutations, rejecting the faulty ones, adding all manner of international touches and signature enhancements, but never straying very far from the long-life diet invented in ancient Crete.

Aristedes' recipes are indeed innovative, but they are also traditional. All of them fall under one or another of the seven categories that define all Greek cooking, both classical and modern:

- **Lemonato** (lemon-flavored). The lemon is extremely important in Greek cuisine. It is used as a salad dressing alongside olive oil; beaten into egg (avgolemono) to thicken soups and stews; and combined with herbs, mustards, capers, olives, and various fruits to flavor meat, poultry, and seafood.
- **Kokinisto** (reddened). Long simmering in fresh tomatoes mixed with tomato paste, onion, herbs, and olive oil does wonders to tougher cuts of meat, rendering them into tasty stews. This kind of meat dish is a staple of all restaurants and homes in Greece. It is tasty the first day and even better reheated the next, and its rich sauce flavors noodles, rice, and potatoes. All in all, a friendly way to feed a hungry family.
- **Krassato** (cooked in wine). The Greeks invented fermentation, so it makes sense that they would use wine and other alcoholic substances in their cooking. They favor sweet-tart wines such as mavrodaphne for stewing meat and fowl, and often flambé cheeses, desserts, and grills in ouzo or the grappa-like raki.

- **Lathera** (cooked in olive oil). From fava beans and artichoke hearts to potatoes and the royalty of the garden, eggplants and zucchini, vegetables play a major part in the Greek diet. Aristedes employs traditional partnerings of aromatics, but pan-dries the vegetables until just tender and then scents them with a judicious splash of fresh olive oil (in contrast to the bland, hopelessly overcooked, oily vegetable dishes we have come to know in deplorable Greek steam-table eateries).
- **Stiffado** (cooked in olive oil, onions, and garlic). This is the meat version of lathera, with the addition of aromatic onions and garlic as well as spices (cinnamon, cloves, nutmeg, allspice, cardamom), sweet wines, and vinegars. Its best-known application is in a rabbit and pearl onion concoction, but it also works with beef and pork, even with vegetables.
- **Yaourtlou** (flavored with yogurt). Whereas French cuisine uses an excess of cream in sauces, Greek sauces are flavored and thickened with lower-fat, digestible yogurt. Aristedes uses it frequently. He also makes much creative use of cheeses and curds, often made from nutritious goat milk, whenever possible.
- **Glyko-xeina** (sweet and sour). Various combinations of honey with fruits (fresh, sun-dried, or preserved), nuts, vinegars, and young wines (moustos) often accompany savories as well as desserts. Documentation of the Ancients' sweet-and-sour recipes exists in Athenaeus' *Deipnosophists*, on of the few books of gastronomy that has survived to this day. Aristedes has extended the concept of glyko-xeina to create a definitive yet flexible Greek cuisine.

The Method

Aristedes' cooking method—or the "two pans and a blender method"—is simple. It requires some leisurely preparation (chopping, blending), and then quick cooking in two frying pans and a final assembly. Most of the dishes in this book are ready in about half an hour.

Aristedes' method is a new paradigm in cooking, assimilating the best features of Greek casserole cooking, French sautéing, and Chinese wok cooking. Traditional Greek casserole cooking, long and slow, results in great-tasting sauces and soups with an added bonus of enticing aromas wafting from the kitchen. On the flip side, however, we end up with an overcooked, tasteless, or stringy piece of meat in the middle of the beautiful sauce—all its flavor has gone into the sauce. French sautéing and deglazing of the pan results in a sauce that fuses the flavors of the main ingredient to the herbs and spices used for flavoring, but the resulting dish is often a little on the heavy side. In Chinese cookery, the hot oil in the wok immediately seals in the flavor of the ingredients, and a cornstarch-based sauce is added at the end for additional texture.

In Aristedes' method, dry searing—frying without oil—results in the main ingredient, be it meat or fish or vegetable, being dry on the outside but remaining moist on the inside. This allows the sauce to penetrate the cooked outer layer, and further flavor the food. The engagement of a perfectly cooked ingredient with its absorbed sauce must be experienced to be truly appreciated.

The most important element of the method is the frying. It is done without fat of any kind, which has two benefits. First, obviously, it is healthy. Second, because it seals in the ingredient's natural juices, it provides enhanced flavor and succulence.

This no-fat frying, which Aristedes likes to call pan-drying, is made possible by that marvel of modern technology, the nonstick pan. A good-quality nonstick pan is a worthwhile investment, as it can withstand any heat level.

You will need two such pans for the simultaneous frying of two sets of ingredients (to be fused at the end). And just for good measure, you should also have a deeper nonstick pan for recipes that call for a pan of larger capacity.

In order for pan-drying to work properly, the pan must get quite hot, hot enough for a drop of water to splatter and dance on the surface. It is this high heat that performs its magic, searing and sealing in natural moisture.

The amount of heat you will need to use depends on the thickness of the pan's bottom and the power of the stove. Even though Aristedes' recipes say to cook over high heat, you may want to start your first few dishes over medium-high and then adjust the heat. The idea is to flash-sear the ingredients, so a little charring is both inevitable and desirable. If the ingredients ever begin to burn, lower the heat a notch.

A bit of practice is needed to learn how to agitate the pan—see the box below for the technique—in order to incorporate ingredients that are added during, or right after, the cooking, without undue use of spoons and spatulas. This is particularly crucial when cooking airy items such as fish, which tend to flake and break apart if handled or scraped. Agitating the pan won't injure them as much but will effectively distribute the added ingredients.

The most important aspect of any cuisine is the sauce. In traditional Greek cookery, the sauce is formed during the cooking, using the tired oil in which everything was sautéed. In Aristedes' method, the sauce is added at the end, usually off the heat. For this reason the sauce ingredients need to be blended in advance. The best kitchen implement to achieve this is a hand blender/food processor (see the sidebar).

Aristedes uses a judicious (but sufficient) amount of olive oil to flavor and enrich his sauces. Because the oil is used raw, instead of as a cooking fat, it retains all its beneficial qualities and its fruity aroma, both of which are diminished when olive oil is heated. There is also rampant use of lemon juice in these sauces. Lemon accentuates taste, eliminating the need for excessive salting.

The "Two Pans and a Blender Method" in a Nutshell

1. Acquire two good-quality large (12-inch) nonstick frying pans, one good-quality 12-inch nonstick stew pot, and a nifty little hand blender/food processor. The market is flooded with easy-to-use, efficient, and inexpensive hand blenders; try to find one that comes with a 2-cup bowl. You will also need a nonstick roasting pan, a few wooden spoons and spatulas, a good knife, and a pair of wooden tongs.
2. Prep the principal ingredients. When a recipe calls for sliced or chopped ingredients, Aristedes frequently uses the words "medallions" (flat disks), "nuggets" (cubes up to 1 inch thick), and "strips" (flattish rods). A flatter ingredient has maximum contact with the heat of the pan, which results in fast cooking.

3. Blend the aromatics and olive oil of the sauce, and set aside. There are only two ways of using a hand blender: pulsing for a chunky sauce; constant for a smooth sauce.
4. Preheat frying pans until hot enough to sear. You will learn how hot is "hot enough" after a little trial on your stovetop. Most recipes call for cooking with two pans simultaneously. This is a lot simpler than it sounds. Use the two large burners on your stove and work systematically from one pan to the other, agitating the ingredients or turning them as required. You will find this becomes second nature in no time.
5. Pan-dry (fry without fat) the principal ingredients (avoiding burns). Remember that searing will lead to a little charring, which is what you want to see. To prevent burning:

   • use tongs, a spatula, or a spoon to turn ingredients in the pan regularly; or
   • agitate the pans by shaking them back and forth on the stovetop; or
   • flip ingredients like the TV chefs by simply thrusting the pan away from you and then jerking it back with an upward movement of the wrist, holding the pan at a slight tilt downwards.

6. Add the blended sauce according to the recipe instructions (before or after you've taken the pan off the heat) and stir gently to incorporate.
7. Serve and enjoy!

Essential or Special Ingredients

Cheeses

Cretan gruyère is a medium-aged Swiss-style goat and sheep's milk cheese with intense flavor. It melts very well.

Feta is the most Greek of all cheeses, even though it is made all over the Balkans and in Turkey. As we know it, however, it is Greek, and even its name is Greek: *feta* means "slice." The best is made from sheep's milk.

Kefalotyri and anthotyro are the romano and parmesan of Greece. High-salt, aged, and quite hard, they are often grated over pasta or gratins.

Kasseri is medium-aged, nutty, and cheddar-like, and is an excellent melting cheese.

Myzithra is a ricotta-like fresh goat and sheep's milk cheese, with a deep herbal flavor, low salt, and a smooth texture.

Chilies are not strictly a Greek ingredient. They are used in this cookbook—sparingly, and usually fresh—because they are part of the "Aristedes taste."

Dessert flavorings: Rose water, orange blossom water, and masticha are excellent flavors for desserts, and are available in Middle Eastern and Greek markets.

Dried or glazed fruits, including apricots, figs, raisins, currants, prunes, glazed citrus peel, and grapes have been used in Greek cuisine since antiquity.

Eggplant is such a frequent player on the Greek culinary stage that it often seems there would be no Greek cuisine without it. It has a spongy texture that turns creamy and comforting when cooked. It tends to turn black soon after it's cut, so it is prudent to start cooking it immediately after chopping.

Fennel is the licorice-flavored vegetable that is much used in Italian cooking and more recently in Greece. In Greece it is found growing wild and is used for flavoring fish and seafood dishes.

Figs are plentiful for about a month a year, and then they disappear. Fortunately they dry wonderfully, and come back to juiciness with soaking and cooking.

Filo dough is the paper-thin pastry that we all know as the crust of spinach pies and baklava. Its only secret is that it needs oiling in between layers to come out fluffy and crisp. It is best to avoid wetting it when assembling pies or pastries, because it can turn gummy. It comes, usually frozen, in thin and not-quite-so-thin varieties. The former are for pastries, the latter for savories.

Garlic is another favorite Aristedes ingredient that is not used much in traditional Greek cooking. In most recipes it is suggested to smash the garlic cloves—just crack them into chunks with the side of a chef's knife—instead of chopping them up.

Grains: Two frequently used grains in Greek cooking are the wheat-based bulgur (a.k.a. cracked wheat) and semolina (a.k.a. farina or cream of wheat). Bulgur is used like rice to make pilafs and other savory side dishes; semolina serves mostly in desserts.

Herbs: Parsley, thyme, rosemary, basil, sage, dillweed, mint, marjoram—even the exotic-sounding lavender—Aristedes uses them all in profusion. The quantities given in the recipes can be increased if you are also a fan of intense flavor.

Honey in most of Greece means thyme-flavored, suckled by wild bees from the purple flowers of the thyme that covers the hillsides of the homeland.

Lemon is the second most important ingredient in Greek cooking, after olive oil. It serves with its juice, and also with its zest, which must be thinly shaved off the peel, without any of the bitter white pith underneath.

Mustards are a miracle of nature for Aristedes, and he uses all kinds and often. They are easy to keep on hand as they have a long shelf life.

Nuts: Pine nuts, pistachios, chestnuts, almonds, and walnuts all grow in Greece, and they have been used in Greek cuisine since antiquity.

Octopus is a Greek delicacy bar none, but, sadly, overfishing has made it mostly disappear from Greek waters. Greeks use the frozen variety from North Africa now, and this same product is available in North America. It must be defrosted at room temperature and boiled in vinegared water to barely cover, so that it can cook into its renowned succulence.

Olive oil is the *sine qua non* of Greek (and also Mediterranean) cooking. Greece is a gigantic olive grove, producing enough oil to drown its population, and even some to export. In this book it is used as a condiment, not as a frying oil. It is therefore imperative (gustatorily speaking) that the brand you buy be flavorful, cold-pressed (extra-virgin), and as fresh as possible. (Olive oil is at its very best in the first year of its life. Its flavor deteriorates after that.)

Olives: Greek olives come in several varieties, with the black-purple Calamatas the best known. Roasted or sun-dried olives, crinkled and very black, have a deliciously concentrated flavor.

Quince is an apple look-alike, with a spongy texture and a tart taste. It is widely used in Greece, both as a sweet and also as a vegetable. It is seasonal, and available in specialized markets.

Raki and ouzo are the native alcoholic drinks of the wine-inventing Greeks. Both are distilled from the grape residue of wine-making and are plentiful all over the country. Raki is like grappa, faintly aromatic and of extremely high alcohol content, because in Greece most of it is homemade (legally). Ouzo is anise-flavored and normally available from commercial distillers, with regulation alcohol content. Both of them have wonderful uses in cooking.

Salt cod is a Portuguese invention using a Canadian fish, and the Greeks have embraced it as their own. It is becoming rare and expensive because of the scarcity of cod, but it still shows up in markets and on restaurant menus. Dried salted cod has a long shelf life, but it requires a bit of a procedure to reclaim its succulent texture. It must be soaked for at least two hours, and ideally three, in several changes of fresh water, at room temperature, to rehydrate it and to desalinate it.

Yogurt is the most benevolent and most digestible of all dairy products, and is used to enrich and smooth sauces in many ancient cuisines. Thickened yogurt (strained in cheesecloth to drain excess whey), which some recipes call for, is available wherever Greek products are sold. If you're far away from a Greek market, drain regular yogurt in a sieve lined with cheesecloth and suspended over a bowl. The whey that drains into the bowl can be used in puddings and cream soups.

Mezedes

Aristedes says:

At the age of six, during a three-day wedding celebration in my native Anoyia, I ate half a lamb.

"This one will live to eat," declared my father, who knew a thing or two about eating. He was, after all, married to my mother, Christina, who was the finest home cook I have ever met and my earliest source of inspiration, a source that continues to enlighten me even now, years after she has passed away.

Eating has been my most loyal friend and ally during a life of various fortunes and far too many widely far-flung homes. Food has always served me, has never abandoned me. It is my one constant in a life of endless uncertainties, and I enjoy, even love, every aspect of it.

I adore pastas and rice; I relish seafood and fish of all sorts; I'd trade a kingdom for a full-flavored free-range chicken, and even more for a carefully bred duck; I'd exchange my sanity (or what's left of it) for a good crust around a juicy pie filling; I'd happily slurp down an aromatic lentil or bean soup rather than almost any other pleasure of a chilly winter's evening; I worship herbs, and have based an entire lifetime's cooking on their floral perfumes and their seductive undertones; I treasure all vegetables, be they the wonderful wild greens that grow year-round on the hillsides of Crete or the finely cultivated artichokes from a gourmet grower in a valley of the Loire; I live by desserts, especially if they are filled with excellent custard, like the galactobureko (custard-filo pie) they make in Anavassi on the way to Lord Byron's favorite ancient temple at Sounio; and I get positively dizzy with anticipation at the mere mention of Greek mezedes.

Call them by any other name—tapas, hors d'oeuvres, appetizers, starters, antipasti—mezedes have always been the most fun one can have at the table. Little bites, of various degrees of taste sensation, they are meant to arouse the appetite, or to accompany a drink, or to "tease the mouth" (*"amuse bouche"*) before an elaborate dinner, but they can easily become the whole meal if enough of them are prepared.

Preparing a large number of mezedes for a party can be daunting if one attempts to do everything during a single session in the kitchen. Happily, many of the essential components of mezedes—sauces, cooked legumes, roasted meats, pie fillings—can be made ahead and refrigerated (though it's essential to let them come to room temperature before serving). And even those that must be fried or baked to order can at least be assembled in advance.

In the universe of Greek mezedes, it's the dips that must take first mention. From the simple yogurt-cucumber-garlic combination of tzatziki to the extensively enhanced eggplant of melitzanosalata—dips are the quintessential way of presenting the various Greek tastes and flavors.

For me, there is no more enchanting way to while away a summer's afternoon than sitting at a shaded table, drinking raki (the eau-de-vie of Crete, a firewater made of grape seeds and skins), and dipping small bits of peasant bread into a dish of taramasalata. This is a dip made of carp roe, beaten to a smooth paste with wet bread, onion, lemon juice, and olive oil. Such a simple thing, and yet such a complex and evocative taste, a combination of the sea and the lemon orchard and the olive grove.

Garlic is the most common condiment in Greek dips. In fact, traditional Greek cookery uses garlic in precious little else. Garlic is the kick of tzatziki, and it is the essence itself of skordalia—garlic dip. But like any other good thing, garlic too can be overdone.

It took me a long time to grow out of my memory of the excessive garlic in the most notorious skordalia of my gourmet-formative years. I was seven years old, and a live-in student in a school run along Marquis de Sade guidelines by the priest Pater Bertolis, a brilliant but militaristic educator, and Papadia, his worst-cook-ever wife. Every Thursday she used to make us fried salt cod, which she couldn't really ruin, though surely she tried, but she would make up for its edibility with a side order of skordalia so intense with garlic it gave me nightmares just to smell it.

The priest knew I hated his wife's skordalia and couldn't eat it, so he would surprise me at the end of the meal with a bowl of the vile stuff and a sharp spoon. He would force-feed me the garlic sauce that was still on my plate, and for good measure, at least another four spoonfuls from his bowl.

One Thursday, in a lame attempt to outwit him, I flung my untouched portion of skordalia out the window when I sensed him approaching. He smiled at me approvingly when he saw that my plate was eaten clean, but his approval of me was short-lived. His wife entered the lunchroom irate, dripping with skordalia. A serious beating followed, and some ten years went by before the lacerations on my back healed completely and I could contemplate garlic again. Now, I love garlic along with the rest of the civilized world, and use it in all manner of recipes, liberally—but in moderation.

There are a number of mezedes in this chapter, and all of them work in combination with each other. They come, one might say, from the same place. Make one, or make them all, sit down with your drink of choice (even beer if you must), and have a party. You'll find that some of them are so satisfying, you'll end up cooking them in larger portions next time, to enjoy as main courses.

Taramasalata

Carp Roe Dip

Greece is a country that loves its dips, because dips make for perfect accompaniments to drink, and Greeks adore drinking (they invented wine, lest we forget). Tarama is the most Greek of all dips, as it combines the saltiness of the sea with the sweetness of olive oil. There are two types of tarama on the market: a white, low-salt, delicious but expensive kind, and a much cheaper, deeply pink kind. Obviously the white is to be preferred, but the pink will do in a pinch.

4 oz tarama (carp roe)
1 cup chopped white onion
1½ cups bread cubes, soaked in water
   and squeezed dry
¼ cup lemon juice
Black pepper to taste
⅔ cup olive oil
1 cup water

Blend together at medium speed tarama and onion until a smooth paste forms. Add bread, lemon juice, and pepper; blend at medium speed until smooth. Add water and oil 2 tbsp at a time, blending at high speed, until all the water and oil is absorbed and the mixture is fluffy and very smooth.

Serve at room temperature with pita, crusty bread, or crudités. (Tarama keeps, covered and refrigerated, up to 3 days. Return to room temperature before serving.)

Serves 6 to 8

Skordalia

Garlic Dip

Here's a garlic dip that requires no effort at all to enjoy, and of which Aristedes would gladly spoon down copious quantities. This version uses stale bread to give it body, though Greek recipes often use mashed potato. Two more recipes for skordalia may be found in the two salt cod recipes on pages 130 and 131.

2 cups chunks of day-old bread, crust trimmed
8 cloves garlic, chopped
½ cup olive oil
3 tbsp lemon juice
Salt and black pepper to taste
½ cup water
Capers and finely chopped fresh parsley, for garnish

In blender, pulse bread and garlic several times until very finely shredded. Add half the oil, lemon juice, salt, and pepper; blend at medium speed until smooth. While continuing to blend, add alternating tablespoons of water and remaining oil, blending until dip has the texture of whipped butter.

Transfer dip to a dipping bowl and garnish with capers and parsley. Serve at room temperature with pita, crusty bread, or crudités. (Skordalia keeps, covered well and refrigerated, up to 3 days. Return to room temperature before serving.)

Serves 6 to 8

Melitzanosalata

Eggplant Dip

Whipped seasoned eggplant is a favorite taste treat of the eastern Mediterranean, and there are as many versions of it as the culinary imagination can conjure. Here's a lively version with which Aristedes has pleased the diverse palates of multitudes over the decades.

For other eggplant salad recipes, see Eggplant "Custard" with Crab on Fennel on page 26 and Pan-dried Eggplant and Beef Salad on page 48.

1 lb eggplant
Salt to taste
3 cloves garlic, chopped
1 cup chopped green onion
½ cup chopped tomato
¼ cup chopped fresh parsley
¼ cup olive oil
2 tbsp cider vinegar
1 tbsp white wine vinegar
1 tbsp lemon juice
1 tsp each finely chopped fresh oregano, basil,
   and mint
Black pepper to taste
A few drops hot pepper sauce (optional)

Peel eggplant and cut lengthwise into thin sticks. Heat large frying pan on high heat for 3 minutes. Add eggplant to pan, sprinkle with salt, and pan-dry, turning often, for about 10 minutes, until withered, smoky, and charred. Remove from pan and chop eggplant into small pieces.

Transfer eggplant to blender. Add remaining ingredients and pulse several times until mixture is smooth but still ever-so-slightly chunky.

Transfer dip to a dipping bowl. Serve at room temperature with pita, crusty bread, or crudités. (Dip keeps, covered well and refrigerated, up to 3 days. Return to room temperature before serving.)

Serves 4 to 6

Tzatziki

Yogurt Dip

A relative of the Indian raita, this combination of yogurt, cucumber, and garlic works tastily as a dip but also as a sauce for grilled meat or chicken.

2 cups plain yogurt (the thicker the better)
½ cup grated cucumber, squeezed of excess juice
4 cloves garlic, mashed
2 tbsp olive oil
1 tsp lemon juice or white wine vinegar
Salt and black pepper to taste

Stir all ingredients together in a bowl. Cover and refrigerate for at least 30 minutes to develop full flavor.

Serve at room temperature with pita, crusty bread, or crudités. (Dip keeps, covered and refrigerated, up to 3 days.)

Serves 4

Kapama

Feta Cheese Dip

This perky cheese dip redefines feta and is widely re-interpretable. This is the one to use for experimenting with Greek tastes and flavors, as it will welcome any complementary enhancement and become your own.

2 cups crumbled feta cheese

1 cup grated red bell pepper

2 tbsp finely chopped fresh chilies (or 1 tbsp dried
   chili flakes)

2 tbsp cream cheese

2 tbsp olive oil

1 tsp ground cumin

1 tsp ground coriander

Chopped fresh herbs (such as parsley, basil,
   coriander), for garnish

Stir all ingredients together in a bowl.

Serve at room temperature with pita, crusty bread, or crudités. (Dip keeps, covered and refrigerated, up to 3 days. Return to room temperature before serving.)

Serves 4

Humus Portokali

Chickpea Dip

Humus is arguably the most popular dip of the quick-snacking set. Aristedes makes it fresh with his own additions, including orange flavors.

2 cups cooked chickpeas

1 cup orange juice

¼ cup tahini

5 cloves garlic

2 tbsp chopped fresh basil (or 1 tsp dried)

2 tbsp lemon juice

1 tbsp grated orange zest

1 tbsp mustard of choice

1 tsp cayenne (optional)

1 tsp sesame oil (optional)

Salt and black pepper to taste

1 cup water (approx.)

Blend all ingredients except water together in a food processor. Pour enough water through feed tube , pulsing, until dip is creamy. Transfer to a serving bowl, cover, and let rest for at least 30 minutes to develop flavors.

Serve within 3 hours at room temperature with pita, crusty bread, or crudités. (Dip keeps, covered and refrigerated, up to 7 days.)

NOTE: To make a delicious dressing for salads, crudités, and pan-dried vegetables, add ½ cup water, ½ cup orange juice, and 2 tbsp lemon juice; blend until creamy.

Serves 4 to 6

Chickpeas, as well as all other legumes, are perfectly acceptable in their canned versions. A 19-oz can will yield 2 cups of drained legumes. If you have the time, you can cook dried chickpeas and legumes at home. Soak them in warm salted water for 1 hour, then drain, transfer to a large saucepan, cover with fresh water, and simmer until tender, up to 2 hours. Drain and use.

Ajika Hot Sauce

This hot sauce of the diaspora Greeks who settled in Armenia is especially flavorful, with its pan-dried sweet apple, peppers, and garlic, and its vinegar. It's a fitting dip for meat, fowl, or fish—in fact, for just about anything. As an old uncle of Aristedes' used to say, "With a well-prepared Ajika sauce, one can eat a whole rhinoceros."

2 cups peeled apple cut in 1-inch cubes
1 cup red or yellow hot banana pepper cut in
  ½-inch squares (or 1 tbsp dried chili flakes)
1 cup red bell pepper cut in ½-inch squares
1 cup green bell pepper cut in ½-inch squares
8 cloves garlic, smashed
Salt and black pepper to taste
¼ cup olive oil
¼ cup cider vinegar

Heat large frying pan on medium-high heat for 3 minutes. Add apple, banana pepper, bell peppers, garlic, salt, and pepper; pan-dry for 8 to 10 minutes, tossing occasionally, until everything is withered and a little charred. Immediately add oil and vinegar, toss until absorbed (less than 30 seconds), and remove from heat.

Transfer mixture to blender and pulse several times until saucy but slightly chunky.

Eat immediately or transfer sauce to a jar, top with a thin layer of oil, seal with a lid, and store in the refrigerator for up to 1 month.

Makes 2½ cups

Croquettes

Croquettes are fried treats that are considered sinless because they contain no meat. Aristedes' are fried without oil, removing even the least vestige of wrongdoing. Enjoy these easy appetizers whenever the occasion calls for something savory to accompany sociability and a drink or two.

Santorini Tomato Croquette

1 lb tomatoes, finely diced

3 tbsp chopped fresh basil

1 clove garlic, finely chopped

3 oz grated kefalotyri or parmesan

OR

Milos Tarama Croquette

4 oz tarama (carp roe, preferably white)

2 cups grated peeled apple

1 cup grated onion

1 tbsp lemon juice

OR

Chios Zucchini Feta Croquette

6 oz feta cheese, finely crumbled

2 cups grated zucchini

¼ cup finely chopped dillweed

½ cup all-purpose flour

Salt and black pepper to taste

4 egg whites, beaten stiff and refrigerated

Dipping Sauce

3 tbsp olive oil

3 tbsp lemon juice

1 tbsp water

Salt and black pepper to taste

Baby lettuce

Preheat oven to 250°F. Place the ingredients of your chosen croquette in a bowl. Combine thoroughly. Sift flour over mixture. Add salt and pepper; stir. Gently fold in beaten egg whites until mixture resembles a fluffy pancake batter.

Heat large frying pan on medium heat for 3 minutes. Spoon large dollops of croquette mixture into the pan and, using a wooden spoon, pat into flat ovals. Cook 2 to 3 minutes, until bottom is crusted and mixture is firming. Turn and cook other side for 2 to 3 minutes, until crusted but still soft in the center. Transfer croquettes as cooked to a baking sheet and keep warm in the oven. Repeat until all the croquettes are cooked. (You should have 8 croquettes.)

Meanwhile, whisk together oil, lemon juice, and water until emulsified. Add salt and pepper to taste.

Serve the croquettes on baby greens, with the lemon-oil emulsion on the side as a dipping sauce.

Serves 4

Saganaki

Fried Cheese

Lightly coated cheese cooked until melted but still retaining its shape is a favorite of the Greek festive table. This version, true to the mandate of this book, is fried without oil and dressed simply. It regales with meaningful mouthfuls, while sparing us the embarrassing spectacle of waiters incinerating the thing with flaming vodka while yelling "Opa, opa!" as happens at opportunistic restaurants.

2 cups water
½ cup all-purpose flour
2 eggs
1-lb block Greek cheese (kasseri, Cretan graviera,
    kefalotyri, or feta)
¼ cup lemon juice
3 tbsp olive oil
1 tsp freshly ground black pepper
Chopped fresh herbs (such as parsley, mint, basil,
    dillweed)

Put water in a shallow bowl. Put flour on a plate. Beat eggs in a small bowl. Cut cheese into four 1-inch-thick slabs. Dip each slab into water, then roll in flour to dust all sides, and dip into beaten egg to coat, letting excess drip off. Transfer to a plate.

Heat large frying pan on medium heat for 3 minutes. Add coated cheese and cook for 2 to 3 minutes, until bottom is crusted. Turn and cook other side for 2 to 3 minutes, until crusted and cheese has softened.

Meanwhile, whisk lemon juice, oil, and pepper in a small bowl until emulsified.

When cheese is cooked, drizzle the lemon-oil emulsion into the pan, to sizzle around the cheese and be absorbed.

Place cheese on plates and sprinkle with fresh herbs. Serve immediately.

Serves 4

Two-Timing Greek Eggs

Eggs are not a common breakfast item in Greece. They'll get served to children soft-boiled, but most often they are served to lunch guests, scrambled and dressed up in one of the two ways given here, and always accompanied by a shot or two of ouzo or raki.

Strapatsatha Eggs
2 cups finely diced tomato, drained of excess juice
8 oz feta cheese, coarsely crumbled
2 tbsp olive oil
1 tbsp dried oregano
OR
Artichoke Eggs
6 canned or cooked baby artichokes, cut into ¼-inch
　strips
½ cup chopped green onion
¼ cup chopped fresh dillweed
2 tbsp olive oil

8 eggs
½ cup plain yogurt
Salt to taste
Thinly sliced cucumber and freshly ground black
　pepper, for garnish

Heat large frying pan on high heat for 3 minutes. Add ingredients from your choice above. Stir-fry for 3 to 4 minutes, until mixture is shiny and cooked through.

Meanwhile, lightly beat eggs, yogurt, and salt in a small bowl.

Add egg mixture to frying pan and cook, stirring constantly with a wooden spoon, for 2 to 3 minutes or until eggs are scrambled to your desired consistency.

Garnish with cucumber and black pepper. Serve immediately with rusks or crusty bread.

Serves 4

Eggplant "Custard" with Crab on Fennel

This is a multipurpose recipe. It can be served as written for an appetizing opening course. The crab can also be mixed into the custard to make a novel dip for a party. The same eggplant-crab mixture can be heaped onto small rusks or savory biscuits to present as canapés at the start of a celebratory meal.

8 oz eggplant
½ tsp salt
¼ cup pomegranate or cranberry juice
3 tbsp olive oil
2 tbsp chopped fresh mint (or 1 tbsp dried)
2 tbsp apple juice or water
1 tbsp whole-grain or Dijon mustard
1 tbsp green peppercorns
2 bulbs fennel
6 oz cooked crab meat or peeled, cooked baby
   shrimp
1 tbsp lime juice
Eight 2-inch spears fresh chives, for garnish
Fresh pomegranate seeds, for garnish

Peel eggplant and cut lengthwise into long ¼-inch-thick sticks. Heat large frying pan on high heat for 3 minutes. Add eggplant, sprinkle with salt, and pan-dry, turning once, for 8 to 10 minutes or until tender, withered, and somewhat charred.

Transfer to blender. Add pomegranate juice, 2 tbsp of the oil, mint, apple juice, mustard, and half the peppercorns. Blend until smooth. Set aside.

Trim stalks from fennel bulbs and cut fennel in half lengthwise. You will notice that the cut sides of the fennel have the shape of musical harps. Carefully cut thin slices to obtain 12 or more "harps." Arrange 3 slices as a bed on each plate.

Top each "harp" with a tablespoon of eggplant custard. Top the custards with a hillock of crab meat. Stir together lime juice and remaining 1 tbsp oil, and drizzle over the crab. Stick 2 spears of chive into the crab to resemble shellfish antennae. Garnish with pomegranate seeds and the rest of the peppercorns and serve immediately.

Serves 4

Tangerine Salmon with Two Peppercorns

Marinated salmon became all the rage when we fell in love with Swedish-style gravlax, which made quite a dent in the popularity of smoked salmon. This aromatic version requires next to no time to prepare and is scented with sweet tangerine as well as exotic peppercorns.

1 cup tangerine or clementine juice
¼ cup chopped fresh mint
2 tbsp chopped fresh basil
¼ cup white wine vinegar
¼ cup olive oil
1 tsp each pink and green peppercorns
Salt and black pepper to taste
12 oz skinless salmon fillet, cut in
   ¼-inch-thick slices
24 thin slices cucumber
1 cup grated daikon
Fresh chives cut in 2-inch spears, for garnish

In a bowl, stir together tangerine juice, mint, basil, vinegar, 2 tbsp of the oil, pink and green peppercorns, salt, and pepper. Pour marinade into a large, deep platter. Place salmon in a single layer in the marinade, which will, ideally, just about cover it. Let marinate at room temperature for up to 15 minutes, turning salmon once if marinade doesn't quite cover it.

   Arrange a bed of cucumber slices on salad plates. Top with a layer of salmon slices, and spoon some marinade around it. Drizzle with about 1 tsp oil per plate; mound ¼ cup of daikon in the middle of each plate and plant spears of chives in it. Serve immediately.

Serves 4

Tuna Lakerda with Honey Mustard

Lakerda is a traditional marinated tuna, which here benefits from refreshingly brief marination and an attractive presentation on slices of fresh fennel.

½ cup lemon juice
¼ cup horseradish mustard
¼ cup honey
¼ cup olive oil
2 tbsp water
½ tsp cayenne (optional)
Salt and black pepper to taste
12 oz skinless tuna or bonito fillet, cut in
   ¼-inch-thick slices
2 bulbs fennel
Black and/or white sesame seeds, for garnish

In a bowl, stir together lemon juice, mustard, honey, oil, water, optional cayenne, salt, and pepper. Pour marinade into a large, deep platter. Place tuna in a single layer in the marinade, which will, ideally, just about cover it. Let marinate at room temperature for up to 15 minutes, turning tuna once if marinade doesn't quite cover it.

Cut off some fennel fronds and set aside for garnish. Trim stalks from bulbs and cut fennel in half lengthwise. You will notice that the cut sides of the fennel have the shape of musical harps. Carefully cut thin slices to obtain 12 or more "harps." Arrange 3 slices as a bed on each plate.

Layer the tuna slices on the "harps" and spoon some marinade around them. Garnish with reserved fennel leaves and sesame seeds. Serve at room temperature.

Serves 4

Calamari with Blackened Garlic

Intentionally burned garlic would be anathema to most chefs, but Aristedes uses it to advantage to enliven the sweet, unassuming flavor of quick-seared squid. This is excellent appetizer fare to accompany wine or beer.

1 lb calamari, cut in 1-inch strips
Salt and pepper to taste
½ cup finely chopped garlic
¼ cup olive oil
½ cup chopped fresh parsley
1 tbsp lemon juice
4 large radicchio leaves
Thin strips red bell pepper or fresh chilies,
   for garnish

Dry calamari strips with paper towel. Sprinkle with salt and pepper. Set aside.

Heat large frying pan on high heat for 3 minutes. Add garlic and cook, tossing, for 2 to 3 minutes, until brown. Add calamari (calamari will curl almost immediately); cook for 1 to 2 minutes, until calamari firms up and starts to stick to pan and garlic is blackened. Add oil, scrape and mix with a wooden spatula, and remove from heat.

Stir in parsley and lemon juice. Arrange radicchio leaves on plates and spoon calamari onto leaves. Garnish with red pepper and serve immediately.

Serves 4

Grèce en Croûte

Mini Pies with Greek Fillings

There's nothing quite as satisfying as a delicious filling inside a tasty crust, and here's a recipe for different kinds of pies you can make at the same time. Even better, they can be made in advance and reheat nicely.

Crust
2 cups all-purpose flour
½ tsp salt
¼ cup olive oil
1 cup water (approx.)

Dipping Sauce
¼ cup green or black olive paste
¼ cup dry white wine or water
2 tbsp lemon juice

Filling
3 cups grated or chopped vegetables (see options at right)
8 oz feta cheese, finely crumbled
¼ cup chopped fresh herbs (or 2 tbsp dried) (see options below)
Black pepper or dried chili flakes to taste

Filling Options
Grated zucchini, feta, dillweed, black pepper
OR
Grated eggplant, feta, rosemary, black pepper
OR
Grated tomato (strained of excess juice), feta, oregano, black pepper
OR
Equal amounts chopped spinach and chopped leek, feta, mint, black pepper
OR
Finely chopped mushroom, feta, parsley, black pepper
OR
Finely diced red bell and banana peppers, ¼ cup finely diced onion, feta, marjoram, dried chili flakes
OR
Finely chopped asparagus, feta, basil, black pepper

For crust: In a large bowl, sift together flour and salt. Stir in oil and just enough water to form a ball of dough. Cover with a cloth and let rest for about 30 minutes.

For dipping sauce: Combine olive paste, wine, and lemon juice. Set aside.

For fillings: Combine well the filling ingredients of your choice.

Divide dough into 16 equal pieces. Dust work surface with flour, and roll out 1 ball of dough into a very thin rectangle 2 inches by 5 inches. Spread a tablespoon of filling along one long side, leaving a bit of a margin. Fold over the dough to enclose filling and pinch edges to seal. Press pie lightly to flatten. Repeat with remaining dough and filling to make 16 1-inch by 5-inch pies.

Heat 2 large frying pans on medium heat for 3 minutes. Add pies, without crowding, and cook for 5 to 6 minutes on each side minutes, until browned.

Serve immediately, accompanied by dipping sauce.

Makes 16 mini pies

Patras Sweet, Sour, and Spicy Wings

Buffalo, New York, is not the only town on earth to give its name to chicken wings. Patras in the Peloponnese is the wing capital of Greece, and the chicken's lowliest appendage is as popular as the town's famous Mardi Gras Festival. Enjoy these during televised soccer games—especially of the Greek National Team.

1½ cups mavrodaphne wine or sweet sherry
1 tbsp dried marjoram
1 tbsp dried chili flakes
1 tbsp brown sugar
3 tbsp lemon juice
12 chicken wings (about 2 lb), cut in half at the joint
Salt and black pepper to taste
Toasted sesame seeds, for garnish

In a small bowl, stir together mavrodaphne, marjoram, chili flakes, sugar and lemon juice. Set aside.

Heat large frying pan on high heat for 3 minutes. Add wings, salt, and pepper; cook, turning, for about 10 minutes, until skin is charred on both sides. Add reserved sauce (it will bubble up when it hits the pan). Cook, turning wings to coat, for 2 to 3 minutes, until liquid has evaporated and wings are glazed.

Transfer to a platter and sprinkle with sesame seeds. Serve immediately with tzatziki (page 19) or kapama (page 20) and toasted pita triangles.

Serves 4

Soups

Aristedes says:

I can never get enough soup. Especially in cold climates. What endeared Canada to me was the deep-freeze of its winter evenings and the endless excuse it gave me to indulge in soups. There is nothing quite as comforting as a hot soup when one comes in from the cold. This was brought home to me definitively during a blizzard in Saskatchewan.

I was driving a dilapidated van cross-country, bringing in a large load of Okanagan Valley rose petals to a plant in Hamilton, to turn them into rose petal jam, a favorite dessert ingredient of mine that exists in Canada only in a hard-to-find and inferior, sugar-heavy version imported from Bulgaria. It must have been about a thousand below zero, reminding me of a physics experiment in which a rose is immersed in liquid nitrogen, and when it comes out it bursts apart in icy-pink shards.

My van, which had been threatening mutiny for a while, finally broke down about a hundred yards from a truck stop. How I survived that interminable walk to the diner, I do not know, but upon sitting down, a steaming bowl of borscht was deposited in front of me.

I spooned it down greedily, as its life-restoring effects washed over me like the gentle surf of Southern Crete, and I became human again. The diner's owner, who had watched my entire transformation from freeze-dried rose petal to fully functional Greek, came over with my main course. He sat down opposite me with his cup of steaming coffee and addressed me in Greek.

The multinational Greek cabal had struck again. He was from Vorizia, a Cretan village very close to my own Anoyia, and had instantly recognized me as a fellow diasporite. "I didn't want to disturb your soup," he said. "For me, there is nothing more important in the eating business than to offer someone a hot soup the moment they sit down. It's what makes them keep coming back. I have truck drivers who drive an extra three hours after they are hungry just to come here and have my soup!"

I have never looked back. I became an instant S.A.—Soup Addict—the most benevolent but surely not the least persistent of my various addictions.

Anyway, as a Greek, I cannot escape soup. It's front and center in all our meals, especially the ritualistic. Magiritsa, an unappetizing-sounding blend of the entirety of a lamb's internal organs—yes, even the intestines and the lungs—along with dill, lettuce, and rice, is traditionally served on Easter Eve, to celebrate the resurrection and the end of the forty-day meatless Lenten fast of the Greek Orthodox. In Anoyia they serve it at midnight sharp, directly after the burning of a Judas effigy and much gunfire at the sky. It is so sensational, such a rare taste, that I make it whenever I've butchered a lamb, which is actually quite often.

Kakavias is the Greek bouillabaisse. Or is bouillabaisse the French kakavias? A moot point, since Marseilles was first inhabited by Greeks, and a fish soup has been the wont of fishermen since fishing was invented. It is what fishermen do with the little, unsalable fish that have been swept in along with the more marketable specimens. Kakavias doesn't have the Gallic elegance of its Marseillais cousin, but it is as fresh and aromatic as the Aegean on a balmy day, and I do give it some extra touches. People have driven much more than three hours to come to my restaurants for the kakavias.

Fassolada, the meal-soup of my people, the staple luxury of the exploited, underpaid Greek Ordinary Man, is a dish I've cherished even when, for several brief periods, I've been a millionaire. Tender beans, celery, onion, tomato, parsley, and a blessing of sweet, jasmine-scented, day-old, cold-pressed Cretan olive oil. This is not eating. This is a soup addict's ultimate reward.

But the most famous Greek soup is avgolemono, a chicken-rice soup that is smoothened with a foam of lemon and egg. I proudly offered it at Orestes, my first restaurant in Vancouver. Being a too-literal neophyte restaurateur, with a background in exacting sciences like physics, in the menu I called it Chicken-Rice with Egg and Lemon Sauce.

Eager to please, I used to make a habit of hanging out behind the kitchen window to watch the reactions of the customers. The avgolemono had gone out to a very stiff elderly man, in a somber three-piece suit, and a silk power-tie decorated (I remember this vividly) with a bold tie-pin with a bird seemingly ready to fly out of it: something that Rhett Butler would continue wearing after his Clark Gable looks had faded and Art Carney had taken over.

He took one look at the soup, took a single poke-around with his spoon, and then, without even so much as a sip, he venomously summoned the waiter and returned the bowl, with the acid comment, "I don't see any chicken. I don't see any egg. I only see rice in some yellow puddle. This is a disgrace!"

By the time the waiter arrived in the kitchen with the offending soup, I was already at work. I placed a whole raw chicken in a tureen, then an entire lemon, several fresh eggs, two of which I broke so they could ooze, then some rice from the soup, and I topped it with boiling water.

I forced the waiter to deliver it, and I watched mischievously as the customer stormed out swearing bloody vengeance. (He was a municipal powerhouse, with friends very high up.)

His bad press didn't hurt me, but the incident did teach me to be accommodating when it came to soup. I have never again described a soup as having ingredients one can't see, and I have put some chicken meat in my diaspora avgolemono, even though in Greece one would get, at most, little pieces of chicken liver in it. And I've never again called its enhancement "egg-lemon," always "avgolemono," and eventually "avoglimono," after a misspelling by a reviewer who was raving about my version of it.

Chicken-Rice Avgolemono Soup

Arguably the most famous of all traditional Greek soups, this has only one peril: it must never reach a boil, or its egg will scramble and separate. Enjoy this one piping hot on a chilly evening. The saffron gives a refreshing twist.

8 cups homemade chicken stock, fat removed
½ cup short-grain rice
1 cup boiled skinned chicken cut in ½-inch chunks
2 eggs
¼ cup lemon juice
Salt to taste
1 tsp freshly ground black pepper
Pinch saffron (optional)
Croutons or rusks (optional), and chopped fresh
   parsley, for garnish

In a deep pan, heat chicken stock to a simmer. Add rice and cook for 8 to 10 minutes, until just tender. Add chicken chunks and simmer at the lowest heat for 1 to 2 minutes, until chicken is heated through.

Meanwhile, blend eggs, lemon juice, salt, pepper and optional saffron at high speed until emulsified and frothy. Transfer to a bowl.

Add 2 ladles of hot soup to the egg mixture, stirring vigorously. Add mixture to the soup in a thin stream, stirring vigorously. Keep stirring and let cook until steaming, less than a minute. (Do not let soup come to a boil or the egg will curdle.) Remove from heat.

Serve immediately, garnished with optional croutons (for heartiness), and parsley.

Serves 4

Chickpea Chicory Soup with Glazed Pancetta

A simple soup made deluxe with the addition of small bits of intensely flavored pork, this one is a good opening course for a special dinner.

2 cups cooked chickpeas
3 cups dry white wine
¼ cup lemon juice
Salt and black pepper to taste
1 bunch fresh chicory leaves, thick stems discarded,
    cut in thirds
2 cups water
6 oz pancetta, sliced into strips or cut in
    ½-inch cubes
2 tbsp thyme honey
1 tbsp white sesame seeds
Chopped fresh chives and olive oil (optional),
    for garnish

Blend together on high speed 1 cup of the chickpeas, wine, lemon juice, salt, and pepper. Set aside.

In a deep pan, cover and boil chicory with 2 cups water for 8 minutes. Reduce heat to medium and add reserved chickpea mixture and remaining 1 cup chickpeas. Cook, stirring occasionally, for 2 to 3 minutes, until chicory is tender.

Meanwhile, heat small frying pan on high heat for 3 minutes. Add pancetta and cook, tossing, for 1 minute if sliced or 2 minutes if cubed, or until brown. Add honey and sesame seeds; cook, stirring, for less than 1 minute, until pancetta is glazed and sesame seeds adhere to it. Transfer to a plate.

Ladle soup into bowls and top with glazed pancetta. Garnish with chives and optional olive oil and serve immediately.

Serves 4

Lamb and Lentil Soup with Dill

A meal-in-one soup to add glow to low-energy winter evenings, this one is chock-full of protein from both its lamb content and its lentils. Some crusty bread and a salad will round it out as a perfect mid-week family dinner.

Ask your butcher to cut up the meat for you.

1 cup lentils
2 lb bone-in lamb shoulder, cut in 3-inch pieces
1 cup grated carrot
½ cup diced onion
3 bay leaves
1 tsp salt
½ tsp black pepper
½ cup diced celery
2 tbsp cider vinegar
½ cup plain yogurt
Chopped fresh dillweed, for garnish

Soak lentils in warm water to cover for 1 hour. Drain.

Meanwhile, heat deep pan on high heat for 3 minutes. Add lamb and cook, tossing, for 5 to 7 minutes, until well browned. Add boiling water to cover and reduce heat to a simmer. Cook for 20 to 30 minutes, skimming froth occasionally, until meat is tender. Remove from heat and let cool for about 1 hour.

Skim fat from stock. Place a strainer over a bowl and drain lamb, reserving broth in the bowl. Cut meat from bones and discard bones. Chop meat into ½-inch chunks. Set aside.

Strain broth through a fine sieve into a pot. Add lentils, carrot, onion, bay leaves, salt and pepper. Bring to a boil over medium heat and cook for 8 to 12 minutes, until lentils are tender. Add lamb, celery, and vinegar; cook, stirring, for 4 minutes. Remove from heat, cover, and let rest 5 minutes.

Serve immediately, garnished with swirls of yogurt and dill.

Serves 4

Kakavias

Fisherman's Soup

Call it bouillabaisse, or caldo de pescado, or kakavias; it all amounts to a delicious, addictive soup that is enjoyed in fishing-village homes throughout the world. Normally it uses up the "scrap" fish, which have no commercial value and therefore end up on the table of those who go fishing. Here we use grouper head and halibut, which are far from scrap but are easier to find at a local fishmonger's.

8 oz quince, peeled, cored, and quartered
6 tbsp olive oil
4 cloves garlic, roughly chopped
¼ cup cider vinegar
5 tbsp water
1 tsp saffron
1 tsp dried chili flakes (optional)
Salt and black pepper to taste

5 lb grouper head
1½ lb boiling potatoes, cut in ¼-inch-thick rounds
8 oz onions, cut in ¼-inch-thick rounds
2 cups dry white wine
1 lb skinless halibut fillet, cut in 1-inch medallions
¼ cup lemon juice
Chopped fresh parsley, for garnish
Homemade croutons

Boil quince in water for 15 to 20 minutes, until tender. Drain and transfer to blender. Add 2 tbsp of the oil, garlic, vinegar, water, saffron, optional chili flakes, salt, and pepper. Blend until smooth. Set aside.

In a deep pot, cover grouper head with salted water. Bring to a boil on high heat. Reduce heat and lightly boil for 20 to 30 minutes, until head begins to come apart, occasionally skimming any froth that rises to the surface.

Place a strainer over a bowl and strain head, reserving broth in the bowl. Set aside flesh from head (especially the cheek), and discard bones and skin. Skim fat from surface of broth.

In a soup pot, layer potatoes, onions, salt, and pepper. Add fish broth and wine. Bring to a boil on high heat and boil for 6 minutes. Add halibut and simmer for 5 to 6 minutes, until potato is breaking apart and fish is cooked. Stir in lemon juice and remove from heat. Stir in grouper flesh and remaining 4 tbsp oil. Cover and let rest for 5 minutes.

Ladle into soup plates and garnish with parsley. Arrange croutons and a dollop of quince sauce on side plates. Serve immediately.

Serves 6 to 8

Trio of Cretan Melon Soups

Crete, like most Greek islands, becomes a storehouse of all manner of melons in the summer. These three soups are Aristedes' tribute to that bounty. They are all meant to use sun-ripened melons and be enjoyed ice-cold on a hot summer day.

10 cups honeydew, watermelon, or cantaloupe cut in ½-inch cubes

½ cup Cretan raki or grappa (or 2 tbsp lemon juice)

8 ice cubes

Salt to taste

Appropriate sauce for garnish (recipes follow)

Reserve 2 cups melon cubes. Blend remaining melon with raki, ice cubes, and salt at high speed until smooth. Stir in reserved melon cubes. Chill until cold.

Ladle soup into summery soup bowls. Garnish decoratively with appropriate sauce and serve cold.

Serves 4

Garnish for Honeydew Soup

1 cup plain yogurt

¼ cup chopped fresh mint

1 tbsp honey

1 tsp freshly ground pink peppercorns

4 slices prosciutto, each cut into 3 long strips

Combine yogurt, mint, and honey. Add a dollop in the middle of the soup and sprinkle with freshly ground pink peppercorns. Curve strips of prosciutto around yogurt.

Garnish for Watermelon Soup

½ cup water

½ cup granulated sugar

¼ cup fresh ginger cut in thin matchsticks

1 tbsp lemon juice

½ cup parmesan shavings

Bring water and sugar to a boil in a small pot. Add ginger, reduce heat to medium-low, and simmer for 6 to 8 minutes, until thickly syrupy and ginger is soft. (Do not let sugar darken and caramelize. If it begins to, add a little water and stir.) Stir in lemon juice and remove from heat. Add as a swirl on the soup and decorate with parmesan shavings.

Garnish for Cantaloupe Soup

¼ cup balsamic vinegar

2 tbsp chopped fresh basil

4 tbsp sour cream

4 tbsp grated daikon

Combine balsamic vinegar and basil. Add as a swirl on the soup and top with dollop of sour cream and grated daikon.

Fassolada

Greek Bean Soup

All Greeks like bean soup, because we have all eaten it from infancy. Bean soup is the most economical of meal-soups, and all households, regardless of their wealth, cook it for a convenient weeknight dinner. It can be made in advance and reheated; in fact, it is better the next day.

1½ cups diced yellow onion
8 cloves garlic, chopped
6 cups tomatoes cut in ½-inch cubes
3 cups water
2 cups cooked white kidney beans
1 cup thinly sliced carrots
3 bay leaves
1 tbsp dried chili flakes (optional)
Salt and black pepper to taste
½ cup diced celery
½ cup roughly chopped celery leaves
½ cup roughly chopped fresh parsley
6 tbsp olive oil
12 anchovy fillets
6 oz feta cheese
12 black or green olives (preferably Greek)
½ cup diced Spanish onion

Heat deep pan on high heat for 3 minutes. Add yellow onion and garlic; cook, stirring, for 2 to 3 minutes, until onions are transparent. Add tomatoes and water; bring to a boil, stirring. Add beans, carrots, bay leaves, optional chili flakes, salt, and pepper. Cook, stirring occasionally, for 6 minutes.

Reduce heat to medium. Stir in celery, celery leaves, and parsley; simmer for about 6 minutes, stirring occasionally, until vegetables are tender. Stir in oil and remove from heat. Cover and let rest for 5 minutes.

Serve with a side plate of anchovies, feta, olives, and sweet onion for garnishes.

Serves 6

Drunken Dako Tomato Soup

Dako, the signature appetizer of Crete, is a salad of wet barley rusk topped with tomato, goat cheese, and olive oil. It goes excellently with raki. Aristedes here turns it into a soup, made lively with a shot of booze. This is generally a room-temperature soup, but you can serve it hot if you prefer. Simply bring the soup to a boil before garnishing.

10 cups ripe summer tomatoes cut in ¼-inch dice
½ cup Cretan raki or grappa
¼ cup olive oil
1 tbsp dried oregano
Salt and black pepper to taste
4 large rusks (barley, whole wheat, or rye)
4 oz Cretan myzithra or soft goat cheese
12 Calamata olives, pitted and halved
1 tbsp drained capers
Fresh chives cut in ½-inch spears, for garnish

In blender, blend half the tomatoes on high until smooth. Transfer to a bowl and add remaining tomatoes, raki, oil, oregano, salt, and pepper. Mix well.

Ladle soup into bowls. Place rusk in the middle. Top each rusk with a scoop of goat cheese and some olives and capers. Garnish generously with chives. Serve at room temperature.

Serves 4

Giouvarlakia

Meatball Soup

This dish, with its blandness and its rubbery meatballs, was often administered to children as an all-purpose punishment, and even better as a deterrent (as in "I'll make giouvarlakia!"). This recipe lightens the texture (with bulgur) and adds interesting aromatics. Doesn't mean children will hate it any less, but adults will find it surprisingly enjoyable.

2 cups instant bulgur (cracked wheat)
½ cup cold water
1 lb lean ground beef
1 cup finely chopped onion
½ cup finely chopped fresh parsley
2 tbsp chopped pine nuts
2 tbsp olive oil
1 tbsp each dried thyme and marjoram
Salt and black pepper to taste
6 cups boiling water
2 cups coarsely chopped tomatoes
1 cup thinly sliced leeks
1 cup dry white wine
2 eggs
¼ cup lemon juice
Additional chopped fresh parsley, for garnish

Combine bulgur with cold water; let stand a few minutes until bulgur has absorbed water. Add beef, onion, parsley, pine nuts, oil, herbs, salt, and pepper. Mix thoroughly. Form mixture into 1-inch meatballs.

Heat deep pan on high heat for 3 minutes. Add meatballs and cook, turning frequently, for 3 to 4 minutes, just until beginning to brown. Add boiling water, tomatoes, leeks, and wine; stir. Reduce heat to medium-high and cook for 6 to 8 minutes, until meatballs are cooked through. Reduce heat to low.

Meanwhile, in a bowl, whisk eggs, lemon juice, salt, and pepper until frothy. Add egg mixture to the soup in a steady stream, stirring constantly. Cook, stirring, for 1 to 2 minutes, until just steaming. (Do not let soup come to a boil or the egg will curdle.)

Serve immediately, garnished with chopped parsley.

Serves 4 to 6

Salads

Aristedes says:

From a salad point of view, all of Greece is a wide-open greengrocer's with delectable vegetables, precisely vine-ripened, bursting with flavor, ready for the plucking. I'll never forget my first visit to my mother's native island, Milos, when I was six. It was August, and the air was rife with the sweet-sourness of nightshade, a perfume so intense it would kick-start the Sirens' call for my own culinary Odyssey.

I was on donkey-back, my mother clutching me into suffocating safety with an arm across my face, so that only my eyes were uncovered. I was looking at fields on either side of the road with an endless green carpet on which shone countless red balls.

"Red balls, Mama," I cried. "No, no, darling," she laughed. "Tomatoes!" And she got off the donkey and picked one for me. I bit into it, unaware of just how juicy a Greek tomato can be. It drowned me, I gagged, but I couldn't stop eating. It was instant addiction, the kind that keeps you awake at night and will not let up until you satisfy the craving.

I had to wait until I was nineteen for my return visit to Milos at the right time of year. By now other kinds of delectable spherical entities had caught my attention, and Milos was bursting with that sort as well, since it had become a favorite haunt of Scandinavian tourists, mostly female, with a penchant for tiny bikinis whose tops would come undone whenever it was felt no one was watching.

"Of course, every Milian male was watching, myself included, but unlike the rest of those men, it was the tomatoes of the fields that inflamed my palate. It was not just the replay of childhood nostalgia. It was the unmitigated pleasure of a Greek salad (no more mere bites of a nude "red ball" for me). A perfect tomato, in the company of cool cucumber, pungent onion, briny black olives, goaty feta cheese, and a simple dressing of oil, salt, and pepper, is such bravura fare, so astounding a meal on a hot day after a refreshing swim, that no other salad need ever be invented.

And that is why Greeks eat the same salad every day of the long months of their extended summer. And in the winter, especially in wild-green-abundant Crete, they replace the tomato with one kind or another of seasonally growing bitter leaves from the mountains. These are known generically as horta in Greece and as dandelions around the world.

Horta and tomatoes have been the foundation of Greek salad for millennia, but times are changing. Greece is under the spell of 'new' gastronomy, something that I espoused at least twenty years ago. All our traditional dishes are being reinvented, and our salads even more so, since they have become the staple supper of all those wealthy, permanently-on-diets fashionable restaurant clients.

And just like the salads of the rest of the global culinary community, a Greek salad these days is just as likely to contain Belgian endive, or spiced eggplant, or lemony avocado, or sun-dried tomato, or, indeed, chicken or beef or seafood, as it might feta or black olives. But a salad always will be an entertaining way to start a dinner, or to finish it, or even to be the entirety of a light and lively meal in itself.

Grilled Haloumi with Tomato and Arugula

This simple salad becomes special with the bitter flavor of arugula and the particular sheep's milk taste and texture of haloumi cheese.

½ cup chopped fresh mint
½ cup fresh orange juice
3 tbsp lemon juice
3 tbsp olive oil
Salt and black pepper to taste
1 lb cherry tomatoes, halved
2 bunches arugula, torn into chunks
1 lb haloumi cheese, cut in ½-inch medallions
2 tbsp balsamic vinegar
Drained capers and Greek black olives, for garnish

In a small bowl, combine mint, orange juice, lemon juice, oil, salt, and pepper. Stir to form a loose emulsion. Set aside.

Arrange tomatoes and arugula decoratively on salad plates.

Heat large frying pan on high heat for 3 minutes. Add haloumi cheese and cook for 1 to 2 minutes on each side, until soft and stretchy (haloumi does not melt).

Arrange haloumi slices in between tomatoes and arugula. Drizzle lemon sauce all over salad, and sprinkle a few drops of balsamic vinegar here and there. Garnish with capers and olives and serve immediately.

Serves 4

Pan-dried Eggplant and Beef Salad

This salad is a delicious opening course as well as an excellent lunch on its own. It combines a room-temperature eggplant mixture (which can be prepared in advance) with the warmth of cooked-to-order beef.

1 lb eggplant
½ tsp salt
8 cloves garlic, smashed
4 tbsp chopped fresh basil
4 tbsp olive oil
1 tbsp lemon juice
¼ tsp black pepper
4 cups mixed baby lettuce
¾ cup blood or regular orange juice
2 tbsp cider vinegar
1 tsp grated orange zest
8 oz boneless steak of choice, trimmed of fat and
    cut into ½-inch-thick strips

Peel eggplant and cut lengthwise into long ¼-inch-thick sticks. Heat large frying pan on high heat for 3 minutes. Add eggplant to pan, sprinkle with salt, and pan-dry, turning once, for 5 minutes. Add garlic and continue pan-drying for 4 to 5 minutes (being careful not to burn garlic), until eggplant is tender, withered, and slightly charred.

Chop eggplant and garlic into small bits. Transfer to a bowl and, using a fork, mash until smooth but still somewhat chunky. Stir in basil, 3 tbsp of the oil, lemon juice, and pepper. Mound in the middle of large plates, and ring generously with lettuce leaves.

In a small bowl, stir together orange juice, vinegar, remaining 1 tbsp oil, and orange zest. Set aside.

Reheat same pan on high heat for 3 minutes. Add beef and cook, tossing, for 1 minute for rare (longer for well done). Immediately arrange beef on the rings of lettuce around the eggplant.

Add orange juice mixture to pan. Boil, stirring, for 2 to 3 minutes, until reduced by half.

Drizzle the leaves with the pan sauce, and sprinkle salad with freshly ground black pepper. Serve immediately.

Serves 4

Beet and Onion Salad

In Ukrainian borscht, roasted Italian style, and in this Greek salad are arguably the tastiest ways to enjoy beets.

1 lb baby beets with greens
¾ cup blood orange juice or pink grapefruit juice
¼ cup red wine vinegar
¼ cup olive oil
Salt and black pepper to taste
8 oz Spanish onion, cut in ¼-inch-thick rings
2 tbsp drained baby capers (or 3 tbsp regular
   capers)
Chopped fresh coriander, parsley, or basil, for garnish
Grapefruit or blood orange segments, for garnish

Cut greens from beets, coarsely chop, and set aside. Cut beets in half. Boil beets in just enough salted water to barely cover for 10 minutes. Add beet greens and boil for 10 minutes more or until beets are tender. (If using older beets, boil for 30 to 40 minutes total.) Drain beets, reserving ¼ cup of the cooking water. Peel beets and cut crosswise into ¼-inch-thick half-moons. Transfer to a bowl.

Blend together on high speed reserved cooking water, orange juice, vinegar, oil, salt, and pepper until emulsified. Add to the beets. Add onion and capers, and fold until salad is well coated with dressing.

Garnish with coriander and orange segments and serve immediately. (Salad keeps, covered and refrigerated, for up to 4 days. Bring to room temperature before serving.)

Serves 4 to 6

Spinach with Two Dressings

If anything will do justice to spinach, the dual dressing of this salad is bound to be it. Pan-dried tomatoes and minty cheese on lightly sautéed spinach is a salad that could be a complete lunch or the opening course of a full dinner.

8 oz plum tomatoes, halved lengthwise
Salt and black pepper to taste
2 tbsp chopped fresh basil (or 1 tbsp dried)
1 tbsp drained capers
4 tbsp olive oil
Black pepper to taste
4 oz myzithra cheese or ricotta
¼ cup chopped fresh mint (or 1 tbsp dried)
1 lb fresh spinach, washed and dried
2 tbsp white wine vinegar
Toasted walnuts, for garnish

Heat large frying pan on high heat for 3 minutes. Add tomatoes, cut side up, sprinkle with salt, and cook undisturbed for 8 to 10 minutes, until somewhat withered but still juicy.

Transfer tomatoes to a bowl. Add basil, capers, 1 tbsp of the oil, salt, and pepper. Mix well and set aside.

In another bowl, combine cheese, mint, 1 tbsp of the oil, and salt. Set aside.

Roughly tear spinach into a bowl. Add vinegar and remaining 2 tbsp oil. Toss well.

Arrange spinach on salad plates. Put a dollop of cheese mixture in the center. Spoon tomato mixture generously over the spinach. Garnish with walnuts and serve immediately.

Serves 4

Athenian Fish Salad

Poached fish and mixed vegetables dressed with a tangy sauce and garnished with salad ingredients will make a showy centerpiece for a festive buffet as well as a family lunch. Save this one for a warm, lazy day.

¼ cup lemon juice
¼ cup olive oil
¼ cup water
1 tbsp hot mustard (Colman's or Dijon)
Salt and pepper to taste
1 cup potato cut in ½-inch cubes
½ cup carrot cut in ¼-inch rounds
1 lb skinless grouper fillet (or halibut or cod),
    cut in 1-inch nuggets
½ cup diced celery
½ cup finely chopped green onion
½ cup roughly chopped fresh parsley
2 tbsp drained capers
4 cups baby lettuce
2 hard-cooked eggs, cut into wedges
8 black olives
Thinly sliced red banana pepper

Blend together lemon juice, oil, water, mustard, salt, and pepper until emulsified. Set aside.

Put potatoes and carrots in a deep pot and cover with salted water. Bring to a boil and cook for 6 to 8 minutes, until tender. Drain vegetables and transfer to a bowl.

Meanwhile, add enough water to come halfway up the side of a large frying pan; bring to a boil, then reduce heat to a bare simmer (you do not want to see bubbles breaking the surface). Add fish and poach for 5 to 6 minutes, until just flaky. Immediately drain fish and add to vegetables in the bowl.

Add celery, green onion, parsley, and capers. Add lemon-mustard dressing and gently but thoroughly fold everything together.

Arrange lettuce on salad plates. Mound fish salad on the lettuce. Top with egg wedges, olives, and red pepper. Serve within 1 hour.

Serves 4

Glazed Lavender Chicken Salad

A composed salad with perfumes and textures worthy of a special occasion, this one is easy to make but impresses with complex taste combinations.

½ cup white wine or water
¼ cup olive oil
¼ cup honey
2 tbsp chopped fresh lavender (or 1 tbsp chopped
  fresh marjoram)
8 slices lemon, ¼ inch thick
2 large boneless skinless chicken breasts, cut into
  ¼-inch-thick long strips
Salt and black pepper to taste
4 cups baby lettuce
Fresh chives, for garnish

Whisk together wine, oil, honey, lavender, and lemon juice. Set aside.

Place lemon slices in one layer in large frying pan. Add boiling water to cover. Cover and lightly boil for 10 to 12 minutes, undisturbed, until rind is soft. Drain lemons and set aside.

Wipe dry the frying pan and heat on medium heat for 3 minutes. Add lemon slices and brown for 2 minutes on each side. Cut in quarters.

Meanwhile, heat large frying pan on high heat for 3 minutes. Add chicken, sprinkle with salt and pepper, and cook, turning, for 2 to 3 minutes, until browned all over. Add honey-lemon mixture and cook, tossing, for 1 to 2 minutes, until sauce starts to thicken. Remove from heat and fold in lemon pieces.

Make a bed of lettuce leaves on salad plates. Arrange chicken and lemons in the middle. Drizzle pan juices over everything. Garnish with whole chives and serve immediately.

Serves 4

Calamari in Burnt Mustard Salad

Calamari is a versatile seafood that can please in other ways than being simply fried or grilled. Here's a recipe that highlights its sweet flavor and delicate texture.

1 cup dry white wine
3 tbsp lemon juice
1 tbsp green peppercorns
1 tbsp drained capers
1 tsp Worcestershire sauce
½ tsp each dried oregano and dried marjoram
Salt and black pepper to taste
2 Belgian endives, separated into leaves
1 bunch arugula, trimmed
1 lb calamari, cut into ¼-inch rings
3 tbsp mustard of choice
3 tbsp olive oil
Chopped fresh chives, for garnish

Stir together wine, lemon juice, peppercorns, capers, Worcestershire sauce, oregano, marjoram, salt, and pepper. Set aside.

Arrange beds of endive and arugula leaves on 4 plates. Set aside.

Dry calamari rings well with paper towels. Heat large frying pan on high heat for 3 minutes. Add mustard and cook, stirring, for 1 to 2 minutes, until mustard begins to brown. Add calamari and cook, tossing, for 2 to 3 minutes, until tender. Heap calamari on the salads.

Add wine mixture to pan and boil, stirring, for 1 to 2 minutes, until saucy. Remove from heat and stir in oil.

Dress salads with sauce, garnish with chives, and serve immediately.

Serves 4

Eggplant with Figs on Greens

Eggplant is a vegetable Greeks understand. Mostly, they understand that its taste can be infinitely enhanced without ruining its essential nature. This salad is a case in point.

10 dried figs
½ cup dry white wine
2 cloves garlic, smashed
¼ cup olive oil
2 tbsp chopped fresh basil (or 1 tbsp dried)
3 tbsp cider vinegar
3 tbsp red wine vinegar
1 tbsp honey
Salt and black pepper to taste
1 lb eggplant
1 lb watercress and mixed baby lettuces
Cherry tomatoes, halved, for garnish

Soak figs in wine for 30 minutes.

Remove 4 figs from the wine and slice them in thin sticks; set aside.

Transfer remaining figs and wine to bowl of blender. Add garlic, oil, basil, cider vinegar, red wine vinegar, honey, salt, and pepper. Blend until smooth. Set aside.

Peel eggplant and cut lengthwise into long ¼-inch-thick sticks. Heat large frying pan on high heat for 3 minutes. Add eggplant to pan, sprinkle with salt, and pan-dry, tossing, for 8 to 10 minutes, until tender, withered, and smoky.

Transfer eggplant to a bowl. Add about two-thirds of the fig dressing and fold until dressing is absorbed.

Make beds of watercress and lettuce on salad plates. Arrange eggplant over the greens and drizzle with remaining dressing. Garnish with cherry tomatoes and reserved fig strips. Serve immediately.

Serves 4

Octopus and Avocado on Endive

Octopus is now available universally, albeit frozen. Happily, octopus loses little in the freezing process, and, thawed, is just as succulent as the fresh. Here it partners avocado and endive for a salad to remember.

3 tbsp olive oil
2 tbsp lemon juice
1 tbsp Dijon mustard
1 tbsp drained capers
Salt and black pepper to taste
1 lb octopus tentacles
1 tbsp red wine vinegar
2 ripe avocados, peeled
1 tbsp finely chopped fresh chives
12 leaves Belgian endive
Chopped fresh coriander, for garnish

In a small bowl, whisk together oil, lemon juice, mustard, capers, salt, and pepper until emulsified. Set aside.

Put octopus in a pan and add enough water to barely cover. Stir in vinegar. Bring to a boil and boil octopus for 20 to 25 minutes, until tender (adding more water if it boils off).

Meanwhile, mash avocado with salt and chives until smooth. Fill the cavity of the endive leaves with avocado.

Drain octopus. Cut into ½-inch diagonal nuggets. Heat large frying pan on high heat for 3 minutes. Add octopus nuggets and cook, turning, for 3 to 4 minutes, until browned all over.

Top stuffed endive with octopus nuggets and drizzle with mustard dressing. Garnish with coriander and serve immediately.

Serves 4

Marinated Octopus on Fava

A hefty salad with the comfort of split peas and the luxury of marinated octopus is an ideal lunch in any season. The "fava" of this recipe is what Greeks call split peas. The beans the rest of the world knows as fava are called koukia in Greece.

1 lb octopus tentacles
1 tbsp red wine vinegar
1 cup split peas
4 cups salted water
¼ cup olive oil
2 tbsp white wine vinegar
2 tbsp drained capers
1 tbsp dried oregano
Salt and black pepper to taste
1 cup slivered Spanish onion

Put octopus in a pan and add enough water to barely cover. Stir in vinegar. Bring to a boil and boil octopus for 20 to 25 minutes, until tender (adding more water if it boils off).

Drain octopus. Cut lengthwise into thin, 2-inch-long slices. Set aside.

Cook split peas in salted water on medium heat for about 30 minutes, until mushy and water is mostly absorbed. Stir until peas have the texture of custard. Set aside and keep warm.

Meanwhile, heat large frying pan on high heat for 3 minutes. Add octopus slices and cook, undisturbed, for 2 minutes, until brown; turn and brown other side for 2 minutes. Transfer to a bowl. Add oil, white wine vinegar, capers, oregano, salt, and pepper. Fold to coat octopus with marinade. Cover and let marinate at room temperature for 15 minutes.

Spread a bed of split peas on each plate. Top with octopus slices and onion slivers. Drizzle with marinade and serve immediately.

Serves 4

Christina's Salad

This potato salad comes from the kitchen of Aristedes' mother, Christina. Its attraction is in the good flavor and simplicity of its condiments, and its touch of luxury is the shrimp.

2 cups boiling potatoes cut in ½-inch cubes
¾ cup carrots cut in ¼-inch rounds
1 cup finely chopped green onion
¼ cup diced celery
¼ cup roughly chopped celery leaves
2 tbsp drained capers
8 oz cooked salad shrimp
1 cup dry white wine
¼ cup olive oil
3 tbsp lemon juice
2 tbsp mild mustard
1 tsp black pepper
Salt to taste
12 inner leaves butter lettuce
8 Calamata olives, thinly sliced red bell pepper, and
   chopped fresh parsley, for garnish

Boil potatoes and carrots in salted water for 6 to 7 minutes, until tender. Drain and transfer to a bowl. Add green onion, celery, celery leaves, capers, and shrimp.

In a small bowl, whisk together wine, oil, lemon juice, mustard, pepper, and salt. Pour dressing over salad and fold gently to coat.

Arrange 3 lettuce leaves on each plate. Mound salad in the middle, and garnish with olives, red pepper, and parsley. Serve immediately.

Serves 4

Pasta and Rice

Aristedes says:

My introduction to great literature came as soon as I had learned to read, from the comic book series *Classics Illustrated*. My favorite was the story of Marco Polo, and particularly the pages depicting the great explorer's return to the court of Venice bearing a gift of Chinese noodles as a present to his Doge, something immensely more valuable than the trunkfuls of emeralds that Polo had also brought.

The popularization of pasta as a result of Polo's travels was quite likely the most important of all the cultural gains of the pre-Renaissance era. Archeologists assure us that pasta more than likely existed in ancient Greece and Rome, but no one can dispute that the thirteenth-century importation of the various noodle-notions of China and the transplantation of the tomato from the Americas two hundred years later initiated an eating trend in Italy that shows no sign of ever abating.

The Italians can rightfully claim pasta hegemony, but the Greeks aren't exactly far behind. Pasta is arguably a vestige of the various Venetian occupations of Greek locations, such as their hundred years in Crete, but the fact remains that Greeks today eat as much noodles and rice (as well as bulgur and semolina and the rice-shaped orzo) per capita as the Italians themselves.

Pasta has an inalienable place on the Greek table, be it the ubiquitous pasticcio (baked macaroni, minced meat, and cheese) or Anoyiani makaronada, the signature dish of my native Cretan village, Anoyia. No Anoyian would let a day pass without a plate of juicy goat-broth-cooked spaghetti with grated anthotyro, the area's prized mountain-greens-fed goat and sheep cheese.

On one five-day visit to see my father's family, I was fed the blessed dish as a starter twice a day, every day (which would not have been so repetitive had the noodles not been cooked to disintegration), but I put up with it, because of the anthotyro. This cheese on its own is magnificent enough, but it becomes sublime because of an earthy curing that results in a multiflavored crust, just like that of a fine truffle. It's the closest to a truffle taste that can be had beyond the forest floor, and at a fraction of the cost.

Half trying to outdo my ancestors, I have invented many new pastas with Greek themes. My most showy is a number I call Pasta Caldera, named for the supposedly dormant volcano in Santorini. It features a hill of linguine, crested with crater-walls of the indigenous white eggplant, where a pinkly flaming tomato-feta sauce bubbles appetizingly, awaiting the slightest breach of eggplant to run lava-like down the mountainsides, which are already afire with pink peppercorns. In another notion I combine peaches with shrimp and angel hair pasta for an uplifting plate that is sure to lead to deeply philosophical post-prandial discussions. At least, it always does me.

If possible, rice—particularly the plump, short-grain variety—is even more popular in Greece than noodles. An heirloom from the otherwise disastrous 300-year occupation by the Ottoman Turks, the successful pilafi (Oriental risotto) is something by which the clout of a Greek chef is often measured. I adore rice, and play with the parameters of pilafi in endless variations.

I will always enjoy a rich gamopilafo (wedding rice), the generic celebratory rice of Crete, especially at weddings. This soothing, filling dish is cooked in the broth of the many boiled goats that are traditionally sacrificed for rural weddings, and normally for more than a thousand guests. Enhanced with goat fat, and drenched in its own cooking juices, this is comfort food of the highest order.

On the other hand, I make perky, exotic pilafs with smoked eggplant, or cuttlefish, or apricots and chestnuts that have yet to be served at Cretan weddings, though I trust none of the guests, save for the most hard-core traditionalists, would object if they were.

"In this section you will also find recipes for raw bulgur (a.k.a. cracked wheat), a wheat product with roots in antiquity that is favored all over the eastern Mediterranean basin. It cooks up much like rice, though it takes a bit longer, and adds its nutty flavor to whatever it is served with. I cook bulgur often, and with great success. It is less finicky than rice, and very nutritious, being a whole-grain product.

Whatever type of pasta is your wont, you can enjoy it with full assurance that somewhere along the line this will have been a Greek specialty.

Bulgur Lamb Pilaf

Comfort food Greek-style always involves a grain, and bulgur, a cracked wheat berry, has been the grain of choice for 5,000 years. A nutritious wheat product, it absorbs the flavors of its enhancements without surrendering its own nutty essence. This pilaf is a main-course item, and hearty enough even for sub-zero weather.

½ cup tomato cut in ¼-inch dice
¼ cup cucumber cut in ¼-inch dice
¼ cup finely diced red onion
¼ cup finely diced hot or mild banana pepper
¼ cup chopped fresh parsley
2 tbsp lemon juice
4 tbsp olive oil
Salt and black pepper to taste
2 cups finely diced yellow onion
10 oz boneless lamb, trimmed of excess fat,
   cut in ¼-inch dice
2 cups raw bulgur (cracked wheat) or barley
1 cup dry white wine
3 cups boiling water
2 sprigs fresh rosemary
½ cup plain yogurt
Cayenne (optional), for garnish

In a medium bowl, thoroughly but gently combine tomato, cucumber, red onion, banana pepper, parsley, lemon juice, 1 tbsp of the oil, salt, and pepper. Set aside.

Heat deep pan on high heat for 3 minutes. Add yellow onion and lamb; cook, tossing, for 5 to 6 minutes, until browned. Stir in bulgur and wine. Stir in water, rosemary, and salt and pepper to taste. Reduce heat to medium, cover, and cook for about 10 minutes, until bulgur is quite tender and has a creamy consistency. Remove from heat. Stir in remaining 3 tbsp oil, cover, and let rest for 5 minutes.

Make a bed of bulgur on each plate. Thinly spread 2 tbsp yogurt in a circle in the center. Heap a circle of the tomato-cucumber dressing in the middle of the yogurt. Sprinkle with optional cayenne and serve immediately.

Serves 4

Bulgur Pilaf with Vegetables and Cheese

Comforting and flavorful, this wheat grain dish and its various vegetable garnishes makes for a satisfying meal on its own as well as an excellent side dish with grilled meat or chicken.

1 cup chopped tomatoes
½ cup chopped cucumber
1 tsp dried marjoram
Salt and black pepper to taste
4 cloves garlic, finely chopped
2 thin leeks, chopped
1½ cups raw bulgur (cracked wheat)
4½ cups dry white wine (or half apple juice
    and half wine)
1 tbsp dried thyme
2 carrots, grated
2 zucchini, grated
1 cup kasseri cheese (or medium cheddar)
    cut in ¼-inch cubes
¼ cup olive oil
2 tbsp lemon juice
Chopped fresh parsley, for garnish

Blend together on high speed tomatoes and cucumber. Strain to remove excess liquid. Transfer to a small bowl and stir in marjoram, salt, and pepper. You will have a gazpacho-like sauce. Set aside.

Heat large frying pan on high heat for 3 minutes. Add garlic and leeks; pan-dry, tossing, for 2 minutes. Add bulgur, wine, and thyme. Cook, stirring frequently, for 5 minutes. Add carrots and zucchini. Cook, stirring, for about 5 minutes, until bulgur is soft and liquid is absorbed. Fold in cheese, oil, and lemon juice. Remove from heat, cover, and let rest for 5 minutes.

Mound pilaf in the center of each plate. Surround with sauce. Garnish with parsley and serve immediately.

Serves 4

Cuttlefish Bulgur Pilaf

This specialty item is for fans of the deep tastes of the sea. Cuttlefish ink, the ingredient responsible for the dazzling flavor, is available powdered or frozen; it's good either way. If you are using fresh cuttlefish, have your fishmonger extract the ink from the ink sac while he is cleaning the fish.

2 cups raw bulgur (cracked wheat)
1 lb cuttlefish
2 cups tomatoes cut in ½-inch cubes
2 cups dry white wine
½ cup fresh basil leaves
1 tbsp powdered or frozen cuttlefish ink
4 cloves garlic, chopped
Salt and black pepper to taste
¼ cup olive oil
1 bulb fennel

Cook bulgur, covered, in boiling salted water on medium heat for 10 minutes, until it is getting tender but is not quite cooked through. Drain bulgur.

Meanwhile, heat a large frying pan on high heat for 3 minutes. Add cuttlefish and cook, tossing, for 2 to 3 minutes, until slightly browned and tender. Slice cuttlefish into ¼-inch wide long strips. Set aside.

Return pan to high heat and add tomatoes, wine, basil, cuttlefish ink, garlic, salt, and pepper. Cook, stirring, for 2 minutes. Reduce heat to medium. Stir in drained bulgur and cook for 3 to 4 minutes, until bulgur is well coated. Gently fold in cuttlefish and remove from heat. Fold in oil. Cover and let rest for 5 minutes.

Trim leaves from fennel; coarsely chop leaves and set aside. Cut fennel bulb in half lengthwise, exposing the "harp"-like inner surface. Using a mandolin or very sharp knife, shave very thin "harps" from both halves of the fennel.

Portion pilaf on plates. Decorate with a ring of fennel "harps" and garnish with fennel leaves. Serve immediately.

Serves 4

Rigatoni with Beef

A hearty, uplifting pasta with quick-seared beef and the pure taste of pan-dried tomato is the ticket to bring cheer to the end of even the most trying day. The bonus here is a tomato sauce that sings for itself, without the use of garlic, or even herbs.

4 tbsp olive oil
¼ cup dry white wine
2 tbsp plain yogurt
Salt and black pepper to taste
10 oz rigatoni
1½ lb plum tomatoes, halved lengthwise
½ tsp salt
1 lb boneless steak of choice, trimmed of fat
    and cut into ½-inch-thick strips
Grated kefalotyri or pecorino cheese
Chopped fresh chives

Stir together 2 tbsp of the oil, wine, yogurt, salt, and pepper in a bowl. Set aside.

In deep pan of boiling salted water, cook rigatoni until just tender, about 10 minutes.

Meanwhile, heat large frying pan on high heat for 3 minutes. Add tomatoes, cut side up, and sprinkle with salt. Pan-dry for 10 minutes, turning once, until withered and slightly charred.

When pasta is ready, drain and immediately add to tomatoes, along with remaining 2 tbsp oil. Reduce heat to medium. Turn rigatoni in tomatoes to coat, for less than 1 minute. Remove from heat.

Meanwhile, heat second large frying pan on high heat for 3 minutes. Add beef and cook, turning, to sear all sides, less than 2 minutes for medium, slightly longer for well done. Add yogurt mixture and toss for 30 seconds to coat beef. Remove from heat.

Portion rigatoni onto plates and spoon beef around it. Sprinkle cheese over rigatoni, and sprinkle chives over beef. Serve immediately.

Serves 4

Pastichio with Artichokes and Fennel

Pastichio is a pasta and cheese sauce combo that is normally assembled at great length and then baked in the oven for an hour until it crisps up top and sets into a dense mass. Here, it takes a fraction of the time and cooks up tender and juicy, but retains its top crust for attractive presentation.

1 bunch sorrel or arugula
½ cup dry white wine
3 tbsp olive oil
Salt and black pepper to taste
12 oz hylopites pasta or macaroni
2 medium bulbs fennel, julienned
1 lb myzithra cheese or ricotta
2 cans (each 10 oz) baby artichokes, drained and
    quartered
8 oz metsovone cheese (or other smoked cheese),
    coarsely shredded

Heat large frying pan on high heat for 3 minutes. Add sorrel and wine. Cook, stirring, for 1 to 2 minutes, until sorrel is wilted. Transfer sorrel and wine to blender. Add oil, salt, and pepper. Pulse a few times until emulsified but still leafy. Set aside.

In deep pan of boiling salted water, cook pasta and fennel until pasta is just tender. Drain pasta and transfer to a bowl. Add myzithra cheese and salt and pepper to taste. Stir a few times to mix.

Arrange artichokes and smoked cheese in one layer in a large frying pan. Gently spread pasta mixture on top, without disturbing artichokes and cheese. Cover pan and place on medium heat. Cook for 5 to 6 minutes, undisturbed. Remove from heat.

Run a spatula around the edge of the pan. Hold a large plate over the pan and turn pan upside down onto the plate. Lift away pan. The pastichio will resemble a large pie with a browned top.

Cut pastichio into quarters or sixths and, using a spatula, transfer to plates. Drizzle sorrel sauce around each portion and serve immediately.

Serves 4 as a main course, 6 as a starter

Agape's Spaghetti with Mint

A summer special, this pasta works only with vine-ripened, full-flavored summer tomatoes. Otherwise, it's a snap. This one is from my sister Agape, who invented it because it is easy.

4 cups ripe tomatoes cut in ½-inch cubes
2 cups roughly chopped fresh mint
2 cups chopped watercress
2 tbsp drained capers
16 pitted green olives, roughly chopped
¼ cup olive oil
Salt to taste
1 lb spaghetti
1 cup crumbled fresh ricotta cheese
Grated kefalotyri or pecorino cheese
Freshly ground black pepper

In a large bowl, stir together tomatoes, mint, watercress, capers, olives, oil, and salt. Set aside.

Cook spaghetti in boiling salted water until just tender, about 10 minutes. Drain spaghetti and immediately add to tomato mixture. Add ricotta and toss to mix well. Let mixture come to room temperature, about 1 hour.

Portion spaghetti into pasta bowls and top generously with grated cheese and pepper.

Serves 4

Angel Hair Pasta with Shrimp and Peach Custard

Sweet and sour, this pasta stretches the limits of Greek cuisine but deserves to be in this book because it's one of Aristedes' favorites. The only trick is to retain the shape of the angel hair "nests," which requires careful draining (best done with a slotted spoon instead of into a colander).

3 fresh peaches, peeled

1 cup dry white wine

2 tbsp slivered fresh basil (or 1 tbsp dried)

2 tbsp lemon juice

1 tbsp Dijon mustard

Salt and black pepper to taste

1 lb peeled cooked baby shrimp

4 nests fresh angel hair pasta (150 grams)

1 tbsp dried tarragon

2 tbsp unsalted butter

Thinly slice 1 peach; set aside. Coarsely chop remaining peaches. Blend together on high speed the chopped peaches, wine, 1 tbsp of the basil, lemon juice, mustard, salt, and pepper until smooth. Set aside. Combine sliced peach with baby shrimp. Add 2 tbsp sauce and set aside. Reserve remaining sauce.

Cook pasta nests in a pot of boiling salted water until just tender, 3 to 4 minutes; try to keep nests together during cooking. Remove nests from water with a slotted spoon to retain shape, let drain, and transfer to a plate. Sprinkle nests with tarragon.

Heat large frying pan on high heat for 3 minutes. Add butter and swirl in pan to cover bottom. When butter starts to color, add nests. Cook until brown and crisp on bottom, less than 1 minute. Carefully turn nests, retaining their shape, and cook until brown and crisp on other side. Center nests on salad plates.

Meanwhile, heat reserved sauce, stirring, for about 1 minute, until hot. Spoon a halo of sauce around each pasta nest. Top nests with shrimp and peaches. Garnish with the rest of the fresh basil and serve immediately.

Serves 4

Macaroni and Octopus

Trust the Greeks to find as many uses for octopus as they can: such is their love for the eight-limbed cephalopod. The dish gets an extra burst of flavor from the octopus cooking liquid.

1 lb octopus tentacles
1 tbsp red wine vinegar
2 cups dry white wine
1 lb elbow macaroni
2 cups tomatoes cut in ½-inch cubes
2 cups leeks (white part only) cut in ¼-inch rounds
1 tbsp green peppercorns
1 tsp ground allspice
Salt and black pepper to taste
Chopped leaves from celery heart, for garnish

Put octopus in a pan and add enough water to barely cover. Stir in vinegar. Bring to a boil and boil octopus for 20 to 25 minutes, until tender (add more water if it boils off). Place a strainer over a bowl and drain octopus, reserving cooking liquid.

Cut octopus into bite-sized nuggets. Set aside.

Heat deep pan on high heat for 3 minutes. Add 2½ cups of the octopus cooking liquid, wine, macaroni, tomatoes, leeks, green peppercorns, allspice, salt, and pepper. Stir and bring to a boil; reduce heat to medium. Embed octopus nuggets in the sauce. Cover and cook, undisturbed, for about 10 minutes, until macaroni is tender.

Serve immediately, garnished with celery leaves.

Serves 4 as a main course, 6 as a starter

Pasta Caldera

The inspiration for this pasta comes from Santorini, home of white eggplant and a (hopefully) dormant volcano, for which it is named. Presentation is all-important here, with the delight of having the sauce spill lava-like down the sides of the "mountain" as one digs into it.

1 lb eggplant (preferably white)
Salt to taste
1 lb spaghettini
4 cups tomatoes cut in ½-inch cubes
2 tbsp chopped fresh marjoram (or 1 tbsp dried)
2 tbsp coarsely crushed pink peppercorns
8 oz feta cheese, coarsely crumbled
½ cup red bell pepper cut in ¼-inch dice
½ cup hot or mild banana pepper cut in
   ¼-inch dice
4 tbsp olive oil
4 large slices garlic toast, brushed with olive oil
   and dusted with dry oregano

Cut eggplant lengthwise into ¼-inch-thick slices. Heat large frying pan on medium-high for 3 minutes. Add eggplant to pan, sprinkle with salt, and pan-dry, turning once, for 6 to 8 minutes, until tender, withered, and somewhat charred. Transfer to a platter and set aside.

Cook spaghettini in boiling salted water until just tender, according to package instructions.

Meanwhile, heat same frying pan on high heat for 3 minutes. Blend 1 cup of the tomatoes until smooth; add to pan along with the rest of the tomatoes, marjoram, 1 tbsp of the pink peppercorns, and salt to taste. Cook, stirring occasionally, for 3 minutes. Add feta, red pepper, and banana pepper; cook, stirring, for 1 to 2 minutes, until feta is starting to melt and sauce is turning pink. Remove from heat and fold in 2 tbsp of the oil.

Meanwhile, drain spaghettini and transfer to a bowl. Toss with remaining 2 tbsp oil to coat. Mound pasta on plates. Shape 3 eggplant slices to form "walls" (like the crater of a volcano—the "caldera") in the middle of the noodles. Spoon tomato-feta sauce into the crater.

Scatter remaining 1 tbsp pink peppercorns over the pasta (like embers of lava descending the mountain). Serve immediately with garlic-oregano toast.

Serves 4

Aegeopelagiotiki Astakomakaronatha

Aegean Sea Lobster Pasta

When in the mood for a splurge (or when lobster is in season, whichever comes first), try out this Greek Island specialty that marries the luxury of lobster with the toothsomeness of pasta and the licorice flavor of ouzo.

Try to buy female lobsters, which are tastier.

4 live lobsters (each about 1¼ lb)
1 lb black linguine (or spaghettini)
2 cups thinly sliced leek (white part only) or
    chopped green onion
4 cloves garlic, finely chopped
3 cups tomatoes cut in ½-inch cubes
1 cup dry white wine
Salt and black pepper to taste
1 cup chopped fresh parsley
½ cup ouzo
¼ cup olive oil

Cook lobster in deep pot of boiling salted water for 8 to 10 minutes (lobster will have begun to firm but will not be cooked completely through). Drain and let cool for about 15 minutes.

Deconstruct lobster: tear off legs and claws. Crack claws, and set aside legs and claws. Pull body away from tail; carefully shell and devein tail. Cut tail meat into ½-inch-thick medallions; set aside. Using a spoon, scrape out green tamale (and red, if lobster is female) from the body and pick out little meats from crevices. Combine little meats and tamales in a blender; blend until smooth. Set aside. Discard shells.

Cook linguine in boiling salted water until just tender, 8 to 10 minutes. Drain linguine.

Meanwhile, heat large frying pan on high heat for 3 minutes. Add leek and garlic; cook, stirring, for 2 to 3 minutes, until leek is transparent. Add tomatoes, wine, salt, and pepper; cook, stirring, for 4 to 5 minutes, until saucy. Reduce heat to medium. Add blended tamales, tail meat, parsley, ouzo, and oil. Stir gently, and cook for 2 to 3 minutes, until alcohol has mostly evaporated. Do not let mixture come to a boil.

Add linguine to sauce. Fold to coat pasta with sauce and distribute lobster. Serve immediately, garnished with reserved claws and legs.

Serves 4

Anoyiani Makaronada

Lamb Pasta from Anoyia

This is the infamous pasta that the people of Anoyia cook to disintegration and get awfully offended if one refuses to eat it (worse than refusing a drink). Here we cook it firmer, and enhance it with sage for a pasta that no one would think of refusing.

2 lb bone-in lamb (or goat) shoulder
1 tsp salt
2 tbsp chopped fresh sage
1 lb spaghetti
2 oz soft goat cheese
Grated Cretan anthotyro or other hard goat cheese
Freshly ground black pepper

Place lamb and salt in a deep pan and add enough water to just cover; lightly boil over medium-high heat for 20 to 30 minutes, until meat is tender. (Add water, as necessary, to always just cover meat.)

Remove from heat and let cool for about 1 hour. Skim fat and discard. Place strainer over a bowl and drain lamb, reserving broth. Wipe pot clean.

Cut meat from bones; discard bones. Chop meat into ½-inch chunks and transfer to a bowl. Stir in ½ cup broth; set aside, keeping warm.

Strain broth through a fine sieve into a bowl. Transfer 8 cups of broth to the pot, add sage, and bring to a boil. Reduce heat to medium-low and add spaghetti. When spaghetti softens, it should be just covered in liquid: if not, add more broth. Cook spaghetti for about 8 minutes, until not quite tender.

Drain pasta over a bowl, reserving broth. Return 1 cup cooking broth to the pot over medium heat. Stir in soft cheese and spaghetti. Cook, stirring occasionally, for 1 to 2 minutes, until noodles are cooked to your taste.

Divide spaghetti and some of the broth among pasta bowls. Spoon lamb over pasta. Garnish with grated cheese and pepper. Serve immediately with any leftover broth on the side.

Serves 4

Smoky Eggplant Pilaf

A well-turned-out rice dish is worth its weight in comfort and pleasure. This one has overtones of risotto without the fuss, and also of an Oriental pilaf without the fat. It can be enjoyed on its own or alongside grilled meat or poultry.

6 oz grated kasseri or cheddar cheese
¼ cup plain yogurt
¼ cup olive oil
1 tbsp dried marjoram
¼ tsp black pepper
1½ cups short-grain rice (preferably arborio)
1 lb eggplant
½ tsp salt
1 tbsp balsamic or sherry vinegar
1 cup thinly sliced green onion
Sultana raisins and toasted pine nuts, for garnish
Grated parmesan of kefalotiri, optional

Combine grated cheese, yogurt, oil, marjoram, and pepper in a bowl. Set aside.

Boil rice in salted water, uncovered, for 6 to 8 minutes, until just tender. Drain.

Meanwhile, peel eggplant and cut into ½-inch cubes. Heat large frying pan on high heat for 3 minutes. Add eggplant to pan, sprinkle with salt, and pan-dry, turning once, for about 10 minutes, until withered, smoky, and charred. Reduce heat to medium. Transfer about a quarter of the eggplant to a bowl and drizzle with vinegar; set aside for garnish.

Add green onion to eggplant in the pan. Cook, tossing, for 1 to 2 minutes, until onion is softened. Crush eggplant and green onion with a wooden spoon. Stir in cooked rice and the cheese mixture; cook, stirring, for 2 to 3 minutes. Remove from heat, cover, and let rest for 5 minutes.

Spread beds of the pilaf on plates. Place eggplant cubes in the middle of the rice, and garnish with raisins and pine nuts. Add optional parmesan. Serve immediately.

Serves 4

Zucchini-Flower Pilaf

The flowers of zucchini (and also those of squash) are the high points of summertime eating. Here they are combined with cheeses, apricots, and pistachios in a risotto-style vegetarian main course that satisfies with its lively tastes and its clean, healthy finish. The dried apricots should be the bright orange variety that are plump and sweet.

3 tbsp shelled natural pistachios
8 dried apricots, sliced ¼ inch thick
1 cup sweet wine (such as Greek Samos
  or French Sauternes)
2 cups short-grain rice (preferably arborio)
1 cup finely chopped green onion
1 lb zucchini flowers (preferably with tiny zucchini
  attached)
1 cup myzithra cheese or ricotta
2 tbsp olive oil
1 tbsp chopped fresh dillweed (or 1 tsp dried)
4 oz grated dry anthotyro or any dry goat cheese
  (optional)

Preheat oven to 350°F. Spread pistachios on a small baking sheet and toast in the oven for 4 minutes or until golden. Set aside.

In a small saucepan over medium heat, cook apricots and wine for 3 to 4 minutes, until apricots swell. Set aside.

Boil rice in salted water, uncovered, for 6 to 8 minutes, until just tender. Drain.

Meanwhile, heat large frying pan on high heat for 3 minutes. Add green onion and cook, stirring, for 2 minutes or until softened. Add zucchini flowers and cook, tossing, for 1 to 2 minutes, until flowers are somewhat withered.

Stir in cooked rice, myzithra cheese, oil, and dill. Cook, stirring, for 2 to 3 minutes, until rice is tender. Remove from heat, cover, and let rest for 5 minutes.

Spreads beds of the pilaf on plates. Sprinkle optional grated cheese over rice. Spoon apricots and their wine around pilaf. Sprinkle with pistachios and serve immediately.

Serves 4

Mussel Pilaf Thessaloniki

Thessaloniki, the "second city" of Greece, is a sumptuous port town with fish and seafood aplenty and a cooking style with links to ancient Byzantium and the Ottoman Empire. It is the place Greeks visit just to eat, and when they do, it's a sure bet they'll indulge in mussels, more than likely in some combination with rice—much like this recipe.

You can buy fresh shucked mussels at fish markets and supermarkets.

2 cups short-grain rice (preferably arborio)
1 cup roughly chopped green onion
5 cloves garlic, roughly chopped
1 lb shucked fresh mussels with liquid
   (or 2½–3 lb mussels with shells, see Box)
1 cup dry white wine
¼ cup olive oil
4 tbsp chopped fresh dillweed
2 tbsp currants
1 tbsp lemon zest in thin ribbons
Salt and black pepper to taste
Pine nuts and lemon juice, for garnish

Boil rice in salted water, uncovered, for 6 to 8 minutes, until just tender. Drain.

Meanwhile, heat large frying pan on high heat for 3 minutes. Add green onion and garlic; cook, stirring, for 1 to 2 minutes, until onion is softened. Add mussels with their liquid, wine, oil, 3 tbsp of the dill, currants, lemon zest, salt, and pepper; cook, stirring, for 1 to 2 minutes.

Add cooked rice and cook, stirring, for 2 minutes. Remove from heat, cover, and let rest for 5 minutes.

Garnish with pine nuts, drops of lemon juice, and the rest of the dill and serve immediately.

Serves 4

If using mussels in their shells, add mussels and wine to large pan with tight-fitting lid. Cover and steam over high heat 4 to 5 minutes until shells are open. Discard mussels that do not open. Remove mussels from shells and proceed with recipe. Reserve some of the shells to stuff with the pilaf for a special presentation (see photo).

Calamari Vissanto

This recipe is adapted from a formula for stuffed squid, mercifully so because it eliminates the messy chore of cleaning out squid tubes and then stuffing them. Here one uses the much more elegant squid rings, which can be purchased at any fishmonger's.

1 cup vissanto wine from Santorini or sweet sherry

¼ cup olive oil

3 tbsp chopped fresh rosemary

2 tbsp currants

1 tsp saffron

1 tsp cornstarch dissolved in 1 tbsp water

2 cups short-grain rice (preferably arborio)

1 cup green onion sliced ¼ inch thick

1 lb 6 oz calamari cut in ¼-inch rings

Salt and black pepper to taste

1 tbsp lemon juice

1 cup formeala cheese or mozzarella cut in ¼-inch
  cubes (optional)

Fresh whole chives, for garnish

In a small saucepan, combine vissanto, oil, 2 tbsp of the rosemary, currants, and saffron. Bring to a boil. Add cornstarch mixture; cook, stirring, until beginning to thicken. Remove from heat and set aside.

Boil rice in salted water, uncovered, for 6 to 8 minutes, until just tender. Drain and stir in remaining 1 tbsp rosemary.

Meanwhile, heat large frying pan on high heat for 3 minutes. Add green onion and cook, tossing, for 1 to 2 minutes, until transparent. Add calamari rings, salt, and pepper. Cook, stirring, for 2 minutes.

Add cooked rice and half of the vissanto sauce. Cook, stirring, for 2 to 3 minutes, until well mixed and rice is cooked through. Stir in lemon juice and remove from heat. Fold in optional cheese, cover, and let rest for 5 minutes.

Spread beds of the pilaf on plates and drizzle the remaining sauce around it. Garnish with chives and serve immediately.

Serves 4

Gamopilafo

Cretan Wedding Rice

The normal recipe for this rice dish serves 2,000, the usual number of guests at a wedding in Crete. Here you get the small version, but with all the necessary trimmings.

2 lb bone-in mutton (or lamb) shoulder and/or neck
   pieces
1 tsp salt
1 tsp rubbed dried thyme
2 cups short-grain rice (preferably arborio)
¼ cup lemon juice
4 oz soft goat cheese
Chopped green onions, lots of chopped fresh mint
   and freshly ground black pepper, for garnish

Place mutton and salt in a deep pan and add enough water to cover. Lightly boil over medium-high heat for 60 to 70 minutes (20 to 30 minutes if using lamb), until meat is tender. (Add water, as necessary, to always cover meat.)

When done, remove from heat and let cool for about 1 hour. Skim fat and discard. Place strainer over a bowl and drain lamb, reserving broth. Wipe pot clean.

Cut meat from bones; discard bones. Chop meat into ½-inch chunks and transfer to a bowl. Stir in thyme and ½ cup broth. Set aside, keeping warm.

Strain broth through a fine sieve into a bowl. Transfer 8 cups of broth to the pot. Bring to a boil. Add rice, reduce heat to medium-low, and simmer for about 10 minutes, until rice is tender. It should be creamy, like a good risotto.

Add lemon juice and cheese. Cook, stirring, for 1 to 2 minutes, until cheese is melted. Remove from heat, cover, and let rest for 5 minutes.

Spread beds of rice on plates, mound lamb in the middle of the rice, and top lamb with green onion. Garnish with mint around the edges and pepper all over. Serve immediately.

Serves 4

Chestnut Apricot Pilaf

This sweet-savory rice concoction works well on its own as a pasta course as well as alongside chicken or duck.

If fresh chestnuts aren't available, you can use the bottled roasted ones.

8 oz chestnuts, boiled, peeled, and skinned
1 cup plain yogurt or whole milk
Salt and black pepper to taste
2 cups short-grain rice (preferably arborio)
12 dried apricots
2 cups water
¼ cup lemon juice
2 tbsp grated fresh ginger
2 tbsp honey
1 cup finely chopped green onion
¼ cup pine nuts
¼ cup olive oil
Chopped fresh mint, for garnish

Mash chestnuts, yogurt, salt, and pepper in a bowl until smooth. Set aside.

Boil rice in salted water, uncovered, for 6 to 8 minutes, until just tender. Drain.

Meanwhile, in a saucepan, combine apricots, water, lemon juice, ginger, and honey. Cook over high heat for about 10 minutes, until apricots have swollen and water is reduced and syrupy. Set aside.

Heat large frying pan on medium heat for 3 minutes. Add green onion and pine nuts; cook, stirring, for 2 to 3 minutes, until onion is softened. Add cooked rice and pepper to taste; cook, folding, for 3 to 4 minutes, until rice is fluffed and drying. Remove from heat and stir in oil. Cover and let rest for 5 minutes.

Spread beds of the pilaf on plates. Spoon chestnut sauce in the middle. Arrange 3 apricots around chestnut sauce, and drizzle some apricot syrup around rice. Garnish with mint and serve immediately.

Serves 4

Breads and Pies

Aristedes says:

Bread is more than the staff of life in Greece; it is what makes eating the tasty, restorative, lusty experience it must be in order to entice the appetite and nourish the person. A Greek cannot possibly enjoy a meal unless there is bread to go with it, to dunk into sauces and soups, to balance with its substance and its familiarity the sweet-salty-spicy tastes of the main dishes, and to fill the stomach. Good fresh bread is to Greece what a 16-ounce perfectly charbroiled steak is to North America: a satisfying meal that can be enjoyed with just enough else to round it out.

And when it comes to bread, there is nothing quite like the kind that one makes oneself, cooked just before dinner, perfuming the kitchen, and arriving at the table with some steam still hovering inside, waiting to be released when the crust is broken. For the home kitchen, my quick breads require minimal proofing and "bake" puffy and wholesome after a few minutes in a frying pan. Try them; you might well forgo store-bought bread, choosing instead to cook up your own from time to time, and eventually, who knows, every day.

The only dishes that Greeks eat without bread are the savory pies that proliferate in Greek cuisine. Then again, just about every person in the world loves pies.

In South Africa, where I spent my childhood, my very first pie craze was a steak-and-kidney named Perk's after the company that made it. I discovered Perk's pies in the fish-and-chips shop my father opened when we first got to Johannesburg. It was a lovely item, with a moist, meaty filling and just the right crisp of crunch in its crust. It became currency for me, and my father would pay me in Perk's when I performed some service in the shop. It was hard-earned stuff, because I used to devour a whole pie in two bites.

At university in England, I graduated to the pub version of steak-and-kidney (not nearly as good as Perk's), and also to the samosa, courtesy of the plenitude of Indian food in Sheffield. The samosa's sumptuous marriage of exorbitant spice and aromatics with simple potato was such a revelation that it opened avenues of pie adventure I hadn't yet imagined.

Now that I've eaten my way around the globe several times, I still see life as an unassuming little package gift-wrapped in crusted dough, with miracles of taste, like holiday presents, lurking within: a pie. I've done spring rolls, and tortilla-tacos, and pigeon b'steeya, and coulibiac, and tourtière; I've time-warped back to Perk's; and I've finally returned home to filo dough.

When it comes to pies, Greeks go one step further than any other nation. For most, only certain combinations are pie-worthy. For us, anything and everything can be encased in crust to become pie. En croûte could well be our middle name. The croûte we love the best is filo, a plain construction of flour and water rolled into thin sheets and meant to be brushed with oil or butter, layered, wrapped around something delicious, and baked.

Filo comes in various thicknesses. The very thin, paper-light variety is used for desserts. The thicker kinds (horiatiko, and the thickest, a puff pastry called sfoliata) work better for savory fillings, of which the choice is endless, from the classic spinach and feta pie, to the famed wild-green kaltsounia of Crete, all the way to my own inventions of crust around main-course items such as beef, chicken, or rabbit.

I've also formulated a one-step olive-oil crust that is used in a single layer of the maximum thinness that can be achieved at home with a rolling pin. It replaces filo to great advantage, compensating for the loss of filo's fluffy layers with substance and flavor.

Pita Bread

It is easy enough to buy commercial pita breads, but there is nothing quite like the freshness and purity of homemade.

 4 cups all-purpose flour
 1½ cups water
 2 tbsp olive oil
 1 tsp salt

Sift flour into a large bowl. Add water, oil, and salt. Stir together thoroughly to form a ball of dough. Cover with a wet towel and let rest for 30 minutes.

Divide dough into 8 equal pieces. On a lightly floured work surface, roll each ball into a disk about 6 inches wide and ⅛ inch thick.

Heat large frying pan on medium heat for 3 minutes. Add 1 pita and cook 1 minute. Press down with a spatula a few times. It will puff up. Do this for about 2 minutes or until lightly browned on bottom. Turn and cook second side, pressing down again, until the top begins to separate from the bottom, creating a hollow middle.

Transfer pita to a plate and cook the rest of the pitas similarly. Serve warm or at room temperature.

Makes 8 pitas

Semolina Cakes

Semolina is the wheat derivative of choice in many Greek dishes, and this Aristedes recipe for an all-purpose side dish featuring it has always pleased Greek diners. Now it is sure to find fans outside Greece as well. Be careful not to overcook the cakes, so as to achieve a moist, smooth cake that will not crumble. This is a good alternative to polenta for those who don't like corn.

2 cloves garlic, finely chopped

1 cup finely chopped green onion

1 cup coarse semolina

3 cups boiling water

1 cup dry white wine

4 sun-dried tomatoes, cut in small chunks

2 tbsp julienned pitted Greek black olives

1 tbsp chopped fresh marjoram (or 1 tsp dried)

1 tbsp finely chopped citrus zest (lemon, orange,
   or grapefruit)

Salt and black pepper to taste

½ cup finely chopped fresh parsley

2 tbsp olive oil

1 tbsp drained capers

Heat deep pan on high heat for 3 minutes. Add garlic and green onions; cook, stirring, for 2 minutes, until onions are softened. Add semolina and cook, stirring, for 2 to 3 minutes, until it begins to color. Add water, wine, sun-dried tomatoes, olives, marjoram, citrus zest, salt, and pepper. Bring to a boil while stirring and cook, stirring, for 3 to 4 minutes, until semolina resembles runny porridge (do not overcook). Remove from heat and stir in parsley, oil, and capers.

Pour onto a large plate or onto a cookie sheet lines with grease-proof paper and smooth out to a slab 1 inch thick. Let cool until set, about 20 minutes. Cut into 5-inch squares. (Semolina may be refrigerated, covered, for up to 7 days.)

Heat a large frying pan on high heat for 3 minutes. Add semolina cakes and pan-dry for 1 to 2 minutes on each side, until browned and slightly crusted on both sides.

Serves 4

Xynomyzithropita

Sour-Cheese Pita

Olive oil crust with a soured cheese heart is an excellent alternative to plain pita for any number of Greek dishes. Serve with one of the dips in the Mezedes chapter or as a dessert drizzled with Greek honey.

1½ cups all-purpose flour
Salt to taste
3 tbsp olive oil
½ cup (approx.) water
4 oz myzithra cheese or ricotta
2 tbsp lemon juice
Black pepper to taste

Sift flour and salt into a bowl. Stir in the oil. Stir in half the water, and continue stirring in water, a little at a time, until a ball of dough forms. Cover with a cloth and let rest for 15 minutes.

Stir together cheese, lemon juice, and salt and pepper to taste in a small bowl. Set aside.

Lightly flour a work surface. Divide dough in half and roll each half into a circle about 10 inches wide. Spread cheese mixture on one of the sheets, leaving a margin of about 1-inch all around. Cover with the second sheet of dough, pinching the edges to seal. Dust top lightly with flour, and pat down with your hands. Roll with a rolling pin until thinner and about 12 inches wide.

Heat large frying pan on medium heat for 3 minutes. Add pita and cook for 5 minutes or until bottom is brown. Turn and cook second side for 5 minutes or until brown. Serve immediately (or later, reheated), cut into strips or wedges.

Serves 4

Pan-fried Cretan Spanakoprassopita

Spinach-leek-feta pie in filo dough has become as ubiquitous around the world as pizza or burgers, but here, for the first time, is a version that uses only a tiny amount of oil.

Replacing the cumin with ¼ cup chopped fresh dillweed will result in the more well-known mainland version of spinach pie.

1 lb fresh spinach
1 tsp salt
2 cups leeks cut in ¼-inch rounds
6 oz feta cheese, coarsely crumbled
2 tbsp olive oil (plus additional for brushing)
1 tbsp sultana raisins
1 tbsp ground cumin
½ tsp black pepper
4 sheets thin filo dough

Tear spinach and place in a bowl. Sprinkle with salt. Let wilt for a few minutes.

Heat large frying pan on high heat for 3 minutes. Add leeks and cook, stirring, for 1 to 2 minutes, until transparent. Add spinach and cook, folding, for 1 to 2 minutes, until slightly wilted. Remove from heat. Drain off accumulated liquid by tilting pan and pressing down on spinach.

Fold in feta, oil, raisins, cumin, and pepper. (Mixture can be set aside at room temperature for up to 2 hours.)

Preheat oven to 350°F. Lay out a sheet of filo on a dry work surface. Place one quarter of the spinach mixture in the middle of the top third of the filo. Flatten it to a 5-inch by 3-inch rectangle, leaving a 2-inch margin at the top. Fold over the top flap, and fold in the two side flaps. Using a pastry brush, lightly oil the flaps. Now roll the stuffed part over the folds, until you have formed a 6-inch by 4-inch envelope-shaped pie. Lightly brush both sides of pie with oil and transfer to a nonstick baking sheet, seam side down. Repeat with the remaining filo and filling to make 4 pies.

Bake pies for 8 to 10 minutes, until golden but not quite brown. Serve immediately.

Serves 4

Zucchini Burek

Burek is a generic Arabic word for pie. The Arabs introduced many varieties of bureks to the city of Chania during their occupation of Crete, but the only one that is beloved, and in fact became a signature dish of the city, is this zucchini-feta version, known simply as burek.

20 Greek green olives, pitted
4 tbsp olive oil
¼ cup water
2 tbsp lemon juice
1 lb zucchini, cut in ½-inch sticks
¼ tsp salt
6 oz feta cheese
¼ cup chopped fresh mint (or parsley or basil)
¼ tsp black pepper
one 8-inch homemade pita (see page 81)
Chopped fresh chives, for garnish

Blend on medium speed olives, 2 tbsp of the oil, water, and lemon juice. Set tapenade aside.

Heat large frying pan on high heat for 3 minutes. Add zucchini, sprinkle with salt, and pan-dry, turning once, for 6 to 8 minutes, until tender, withered, and slightly browned. Add remaining 2 tbsp oil, feta, mint, and pepper; fold everything together gently for less than 1 minute.

Using a spatula, gather mixture together into the shape of a thick pancake the diameter of the pita. Place pita on top and press down to stick to the mixture. Let cook for less than a minute. Remove from heat.

Hold a large plate over the pan and turn pan upside down onto the plate. Lift away the pan. The burek will hold together as if it were a deep-dish pizza, with its pita "crust."

Cut the burek into quarters and transfer to plates. Spoon a dollop of the tapenade next to each burek and garnish with chives. Serve immediately.

Serves 4

Kleftiko

Lamb and Potato Pie

The name of this dish means "thief-like" because it was cooked in buried embers by Cretan rebels fighting the Turkish occupiers. Cooking in the ground made less smoke and thus prevented detection. Here's a recipe for normal circumstances, to be baked above ground in an oven and enjoyed in the safe confines of the family home. Serve with steamed Belgian endive or other vegetable.

2 cups dry white wine
  (or half wine and half water)
2 tbsp dried oregano
5 tbsp olive oil
3 tbsp mild mustard
2 tbsp lemon juice
1 tsp dried chili flakes (optional)
Salt and black pepper to taste

2 cups potatoes cut in ¼-inch cubes
1 lb boneless lamb leg or shoulder,
  cut in ½-inch cubes
1 tsp cornstarch dissolved in 1 tbsp water
  (if necessary)
4 oz aged goat cheese, crumbled
¼ cup chopped fresh parsley
1 lb puff pastry

In a small bowl, stir together wine, oregano, 4 tbsp of the oil, mustard, lemon juice, optional chili flakes, salt, and pepper. Set aside.

Heat 2 large frying pans on high heat for 3 minutes. Add potatoes to one pan and pan-dry, tossing, for 8 minutes, until beginning to brown and soften.

Meanwhile, add lamb to second pan and cook, tossing, for 4 to 5 minutes, until browned all over and tender.

Add lamb and wine mixture to potatoes and cook, stirring, for 5 to 7 minutes, until most of the liquid is absorbed. (If there's still an excess of liquid, stir in cornstarch mixture and cook for 30 seconds.) Remove from heat and stir in cheese. Transfer to a bowl. Let cool for 5 minutes. Stir in parsley.

Preheat oven to 350°F. Cut puff pastry into quarters and roll out each quarter into a 10-inch square. Mound a quarter of the lamb mixture on the middle of the top half of the pastry, leaving a 1-inch margin at the top and sides. Flip the other half of the pastry over the stuffing, lightly press out excess air, and pinch the edges to seal. Transfer pie to a nonstick baking sheet. Repeat with remaining pastry and filling to make 4 pies. Brush pies with a little olive oil and prick the tops a few times with the tines of a fork.

Bake pies for 8 to 10 minutes, until golden but not quite brown. Serve immediately.

Serves 4

Pita Chaniotiki

Lamb and Cheese Pie

Residents of the port city of Chania are big fans of things inside crusts (a.k.a. pies), and this cheese-and-meat specialty is held in such high esteem that it has been named for the town itself. Perfect for those occasions that call for a tasty hyper-dose of protein.

8 oz myzithra or ricotta cheese

¼ cup chopped fresh mint

1 lb boneless lamb leg or shoulder,
   cut in ½-inch cubes

2 cups dry white wine

1 tbsp dried thyme

1 tbsp dried marjoram

3 tbsp olive oil

Salt and black pepper to taste

1 tsp cornstarch dissolved in 1 tbsp water

1 lb puff pastry

4 oz tyromalaka or mozzarella cheese,
   cut in ½-inch cubes

Egg wash (1 egg beaten with ¼ cup water)

Black and white sesame seeds

Fresh arugula or other bitter leaves, for garnish

Stir together myzithra and mint in a small bowl. Set aside.

Heat large frying pan on high heat for 3 minutes. Add lamb and cook, tossing, for 3 to 4 minutes, until browned all over and tender. Add wine, thyme, marjoram, 2 tbsp of the oil, salt, and pepper. Cook, stirring, for 2 minutes. Stir in cornstarch mixture and cook, stirring, for 30 seconds.

Using a slotted spoon, transfer lamb to a bowl; set aside to cool for 5 minutes. Pour pan juices into a small saucepan and set aside.

Preheat oven to 350°F. Cut puff pastry into quarters and roll out each quarter into a 10-inch square. Spread a quarter of the myzithra on the top half of the pastry, leaving a 1-inch margin at the top and sides. Top myzithra with a quarter of the lamb. Top lamb with a quarter of the tyromalaka cubes. Flip the other half of the pastry over the stuffing, gently press out excess air, and pinch the edges to seal. Brush egg wash on top and sides of the pie and sprinkle top with sesame seeds. Prick the top of the pastry a few times. Transfer pie to a nonstick baking sheet. Repeat with remaining pastry, lamb, and cheeses to make 4 pies.

Bake pies for 8 to 10 minutes, until golden but not quite brown. Remove from oven and let rest 5 minutes.

Heat reserved pan sauce to a bubble. Drizzle sauce on perimeter of each plate and place pie in center. Garnish with arugula and serve immediately.

Serves 4

Crab and Asparagus Purses

The great thing about filo is that it can take any shape one likes. In this case, Aristedes has made it into "purses" just to be different and to present something unusual on the plate. The sauce is worth the effort: it lends a perfect touch of moisture and richness.

1½ cups dry white wine

2 tbsp chopped fresh tarragon (or 1 tbsp dried)

2 tsp saffron

Salt and pepper to taste

10 oz asparagus, cut in 1-inch pieces

1 cup leeks cut in ¼-inch rounds

10 oz crab meat (or scallops sliced in thirds horizontally)

1 tsp cornstarch dissolved in 1 tbsp water

3 tbsp olive oil

1 tsp lemon juice

4 sheets filo dough

2 tbsp metaxa or other brandy

¼ cup thick yogurt

Whole chives, for garnish

Combine wine, tarragon, 1 tsp saffron, salt, and pepper. Set aside to soak for 15 minutes.

Heat large frying pan on high heat for 3 minutes. Add asparagus and leeks; cook, tossing, for 4 minutes. Add wine mixture and reduce heat to medium-low. Simmer, stirring, for 4 minutes. Add crab and fold in briefly. Stir in cornstarch mixture and simmer for 30 seconds. Remove from heat.

Pour contents of pan into a strainer set over a bowl. (Do not press down on solids.) Stir 2 tbsp of the oil and lemon juice into the juices, and set aside.

Preheat oven to 350°F. Lay out a sheet of filo on a dry work surface. Fold the filo twice to make a square. Place a quarter of the crab mixture in the center of the square. Fold the filo up around the filling and pinch together near the top (use a little water to help seal, if necessary), enclosing the stuffing in a "purse." Lightly brush some of the remaining oil over the purse and transfer purse to a nonstick baking sheet. Repeat with remaining filo and filling to make 4 purses.

Bake purses for 8 to 10 minutes, until golden but not quite brown.

While purses bake, heat a small frying pan on medium heat for 3 minutes. Add reserved juices and heat for 1 minute. Add brandy and remaining 1 tsp saffron; cook, stirring, until syrupy, less than 2 minutes. Remove from heat. Fold in yogurt.

Serve the purses immediately, surrounded by a swirl of the sauce and garnished with chives.

Serves 4

Tangerine Salmon with Two Peppercorns (page 27)

Trio of Cretan Melon Soups (page 40)

Mussel Pilaf Thessaloniki (page 75)

Hunkar Begendi (beef on eggplant purée, page 111)

Crispy Duck with Apricots and Endives (page 121)

Fillets of Striped Bass with Citrus (page 125)

Prawns Tourkolimano (page 138)

Fig-Ouzo Sauce (with fresh goat cheese, page 161)

Lamb, Minced Meat, and Rabbit

Aristedes says:

What had started out as a quiet day in Ouzeri, my neo-Greek restaurant on Toronto's Danforth Avenue, became suddenly very exciting when I heard by phone that Marcello Mastroianni wanted to come for dinner. Mastroianni happens to be one of the handful of film actors I truly admire, and on top of that he has some degree of Greek lineage. I decided to pull out all the stops, and stocked every sort of delicacy that was within my reach (and in Toronto there isn't much that isn't instantly available, albeit at a price).

He showed up late, after his day's shooting was done, a little grouchy and obviously tired, and oh so ready for some good cooking. I took his order myself, trying to act cool, as if he were any of the other celebrities that came through the place, which he wasn't. After a brief exchange of pleasantries, he pronounced his desire: 'Arnaki,' he said in Greek, his voice echoing the innocent bleating of the newborn lamb he had just ordered.

I was ready for anything he might want—except the particular lamb dish he was craving, a melt-in-the-mouth spit-roast that takes about two hours to cook. On the other hand, I had lots of prime lamb in the larder and a thousand recipes in my head.

I proceeded into the kitchen and prepared all manner of Aristedian lamb with an array of accompanying aromatics and herbs to empower the delicate, milk-fed meat. Mastroianni took one look and roared his disapproval. "I asked for arnaki, and you have brought me meat!" he complained. "I brought you lamb," I countered, "but it's my lamb, my inspiration, and it astounds me that you won't even try it, being such an improviser yourself, the celluloid alter-ego of Fellini!"

"Aah, Federico," whispered Mastroianni, and he finally tucked in. Needless to say, he polished off the plates. He wrote me a note of thanks and an apology, and he came back more than once while shooting in Toronto.

What I wish I had had on hand for him, however, was a baby goat. Sheep and their lambs are commonplace in Greece, but goats are ubiquitous, and much preferred in hilly places like Crete, where they nourish themselves on wild greens and roots, requiring little maintenance, while wreaking havoc on the flora and leaving behind bare hillsides. Nevertheless, in my native Anoyia, goats are the object of a time-worn game of honor.

The idea is to steal a rival's goat and roast it to crispness. Then you invite the rival to dinner, where he would have no choice (as per Greek sensibility) but to praise the quality of the meat, in full knowledge that only yesterday it belonged to him. Much raki drinking ensues, and plenty of innuendoes, and if all of that doesn't lead to bloody murder (all Anoyians are armed), then it becomes the rival's duty to steal one of your goats and repay the favor. Trust me, it's much safer to steal from a supermarket, even with the video cameras and the shoplifting laws, than from an Anoyian.

Minced meat needn't mean just hamburgers. What it says to me is sausage, which is minced meat with extra seasoning and, usually, a ton of garlic (a treat at any time). Frankly, I've never met a sausage that wasn't worth gorging on. This is true even of German wurst, fatty and bland, arguably the least enticing of all sausages.

When I really want to overindulge in sausage, I choose Spanish/Portuguese/Mexican chorizo, or Moroccan merguez, Turkish sucuk, South African boerewors, and of course Greek loukanika, with its citrus-peel enhancements. Naturally, being me, my most favorite sausages are those I invent myself, and I offer you one in this section. It is easy enough to make, since it is shaped and cooked like a simple burger, and I'm hoping you will then invent your own versions.

As for bunny rabbit, what can I say? It has the tenderest meat of any creature, it is the perfectly compact livestock for a tiny country like Greece, and it is the primary ingredient of stiffado, our signature meat-and-onions specialty. Okay, it's the dream pet of all our cuddly children, and the essential nature of our pals Peter and Bugs, but I'm including a couple of recipes anyway for when the kids are off at camp.

Lamb with Mushrooms

A quick, zesty, satisfying plate of rich (but calorie-conscious) tastes and textures. Lamb and wild mushrooms were made for each other, and here they find their common ground. Pound the meat lightly so it doesn't curl up when it's cooked.

1 lb mixed mushrooms such as oyster, chanterelle,
   and shiitake (or about 16 button mushrooms)
Juice of half a lemon
1 lb 6 oz boneless lamb leg or shoulder, cut in
   ¼-inch-thick medallions and lightly pounded
12 cloves garlic, smashed
Salt and black pepper to taste
1 cup mavrodaphne wine or other semi-sweet
   red wine
1 cup fresh basil leaves
¼ cup olive oil
4 thick slices bread, toasted and quartered

Heat 2 large frying pans on high heat for 3 minutes. Add mushrooms to one pan and cook, tossing, for 4 to 5 minutes, until browned. Stir in lemon juice, cover, and agitate pan so mushrooms will absorb juice. Remove from heat and set aside.

Meanwhile, add lamb and garlic to second pan, sprinkle with salt and pepper, and cook, tossing, for 4 to 5 minutes, until lamb and garlic are lightly browned all over. Add lamb and garlic to mushrooms.

Add wine and most of the basil to the empty pan and cook, stirring, for 2 minutes, until wine reduces slightly. Add lamb mixture to sauce; add oil, and cook for 1 to 2 minutes, agitating pan to coat all ingredients with sauce, until the oil begins to separate from the sauce.

Portion lamb and mushrooms in the middle of each plate. Place toast quarters around lamb and mushrooms. Garnish with the rest of the basil and serve immediately.

Serves 4

Giouvetsi

Lamb with Orzo

Lamb, pasta, tomatoes, aromatics: assemble and bake in a traditional clay pot (the giouvetsi) or, easier, as here, cook together in a covered frying pan. Either way, this is comfort food at its purest.

Orzo is a rice-shaped pasta, available in many supermarkets.

1 lb 6 oz bone-in lamb shoulder cutlets,
   trimmed of fat
2 cups leeks cut in ¼-inch rounds
3 cups tomatoes cut in ½-inch cubes
2 cups dry red wine
2 cups water
1½ cups orzo
6 cloves garlic, chopped
2 sprigs fresh rosemary (or 2 tbsp dried)
1 tsp ground cinnamon
Salt and black pepper to taste
2 tbsp olive oil
Grated kefalotyri or parmesan cheese (optional),
   for garnish

Heat large frying pan on high heat for 3 minutes. Add lamb and cook for 4 to 5 minutes, turning once, until browned on both sides. Transfer lamb to a plate and set aside.

In the same pan on high heat, cook leeks, stirring, for 1 to 2 minutes, until softened. Add tomatoes, wine, water, orzo, garlic, rosemary, cinnamon, salt, and pepper. Bring to a boil, stirring. Reduce heat to medium, cover, and cook undisturbed for 8 minutes (orzo will still be very toothy).

Embed lamb in the orzo and sauce. Cover and cook for 5 minutes. Stir once to prevent sticking (if too dry, add a little water). Cover and cook for another 4 to 5 minutes, until orzo is tender. Remove from heat and stir in oil. Cover and let rest for 5 minutes.

Spoon lamb and orzo into soup plates, sprinkle with optional cheese and serve immediately.

Serves 4

Lamb with Greens and Xynomyzithropita

A warm-weather choice, with greens that are bitter and spring lamb that is succulent and tender, this dish thrills the palate without taxing the waistline. And it's ready in less than 15 minutes.

1 lb bitter greens (such as rapini or dandelion),
   trimmed and chopped in half
1 lb boneless lamb leg cutlets (¼ inch thick),
   trimmed of fat
Salt and black pepper to taste
¼ cup lemon juice
¼ cup olive oil
1 tsp cornstarch dissolved in 1 tbsp water
1 xynomyzithropita (see page 83),
   cut into 1-inch-wide strips

Boil greens in just enough salted water to cover for 8 to 10 minutes, until tender. Reserve 1½ cups of the cooking liquid. Drain greens and set aside, keeping warm.

Meanwhile, heat large frying pan on high heat for 3 minutes. Add lamb, sprinkle with salt and pepper, and cook, turning, for 3 to 4 minutes, until browned on both sides and medium-rare (cook 2 more minutes for medium, and 4 more for well done). Transfer lamb to a plate and keep warm.

To the same pan on high heat, add greens cooking liquid, lemon juice, and oil; cook, stirring, for 2 minutes. Add cornstarch mixture and stir for 30 seconds. Immediately remove from heat.

Mound greens in the middle of each plate. Arrange lamb around the greens, interspersed with "fingers" of xynomyzithropita. Spoon sauce over lamb and greens and serve immediately.

Serves 4

Al's Feta Lamb

This recipe was invented and named for Aristedes' friend and customer Al Shawn, who had a deep dilemma. He loved souvlaki but could never enjoy it, as he was allergic to yogurt, a prime ingredient of souvlaki's tzatziki sauce and what renders mere skewered meat into a delicacy. Aristedes replaced the tzatziki with a feta cheese spread, pleasing Al no end while giving hope to the yogurt-challenged worldwide.

4 tbsp olive oil
¼ cup lemon juice
1 tbsp dried oregano
Salt and black pepper to taste
8 oz feta cheese, finely crumbled
8 homemade pitas (see page 81), split
1 lb 6 oz boneless lamb, trimmed of fat and
  cut in ½-inch cubes
¾ cup thinly sliced onion
½ cup chopped fresh parsley
Halved cherry tomatoes, for garnish

In a small bowl, whisk together 3 tbsp of the oil, lemon juice, oregano, salt, and pepper. Set aside.

Mash together feta and remaining 1 tbsp oil. Spread feta inside each pita. Set aside.

Heat large frying pan on high heat for 3 minutes. Add lamb, sprinkle with salt and pepper to taste, and cook, tossing, for 4 to 5 minutes, until browned all over and tender. Add lemon-oregano sauce and cook, tossing vigorously, for 1 to 2 minutes, until lamb is coated and juices are absorbed.

Spoon lamb down the middle of each pita. Top with onion and parsley, and wrap the pita to envelop the filling, securing it with a toothpick. Garnish each plate with cherry tomatoes, and serve immediately.

Serves 4

Maniatiko Lamb with Artichokes

Mani is an erstwhile impoverished corner of the Peloponnese, which has been "discovered" by seriously wealthy European nouveaux riches. This lamb and artichoke stew is a dish with which they used to console themselves before the money started rolling in, and not surprisingly, it's still a big favorite now.

1 lb small new potatoes, halved
Salt and black pepper to taste
3 tbsp chopped fresh rosemary
4 tbsp olive oil
Salt and black pepper to taste
16 thin lamb chops (about 2 lb)
1 cup dry white wine
2 tbsp white wine vinegar
12 cooked or canned baby artichokes
Grated fresh daikon or sliced radishes, for garnish

Heat 2 large frying pans on high heat for 3 minutes. Add potatoes to one pan, sprinkle with salt, and pan-dry, tossing, for about 8 minutes, until potatoes can be easily pierced.

Meanwhile, stir together rosemary, 1 tbsp of the oil, salt, and pepper; coat lamb chops with this mixture. Add lamb chops to second pan and cook for 3 minutes to brown first side. Turn and brown other side for 2 minutes. Transfer lamb chops to a plate and keep warm.

To the empty pan, add wine, vinegar, and salt and pepper to taste; stir with a wooden spatula to deglaze the lamb juices in the pan. Add potatoes and artichokes. Reduce heat to medium, and cook for 3 to 4 minutes, stirring gently, until sauce is syrupy. Stir in remaining 3 tbsp oil and remove from heat.

Mound potato-artichoke mixture in the middle of each plate. Hang lamb chops off the edges of the mound. Garnish with daikon and serve immediately.

Serves 4

Meat Moussaka

This is the signature dish of every Greek restaurant in the diaspora, and even quite a few in the home country. Aristedes' version replaces the weighty béchamel with a low-fat cheese topping, making it frothier and less calorific than the norm. One pund of zucchini strips, pan-dried for 5 to 6 minutes can be added as a third layer between the eggplant and the meat, if desired.

1 lb eggplant
Salt to taste
10 oz potatoes, peeled and
    cut into ½-inch-thick rounds
1 cup chopped onion
4 cloves garlic, chopped
1 lb ground meat (beef and/or pork)
1½ cups coarsely chopped tomatoes

2 tbsp dried oregano
½ cup chopped fresh parsley
2 cups myzithra or ricotta cheese
½ cup shredded Cretan or Swiss gruyère cheese
1 tsp grated nutmeg
½ tsp black pepper
Chopped arugula or parsley, for garnish

Peel eggplant and cut lengthwise into long ¼-inch-thick strips. Heat 2 large frying pans on high heat for 3 minutes. Add eggplant to one pan, sprinkle with salt, and pan-dry, turning once, for 8 to 10 minutes, until tender, withered, and somewhat charred.

Meanwhile, add potatoes to second pan and pan-dry, turning once, for 8 to 10 minutes, until tender and somewhat charred. Spread potatoes in a 12-inch by 9-inch nonstick baking dish. Layer eggplant over the potato. Set aside.

Preheat broiler. Return one of the pans to high heat for 3 minutes. Add onion and garlic; cook, tossing, for 2 to 3 minutes, until onion is softened and transparent. Add ground meat and cook, stirring, for 3 to 4 minutes, until beginning to brown. Add tomatoes and oregano; cook, stirring, for 3 to 4 minutes, until saucy. Remove from heat and stir in parsley.

Spread meat mixture over the eggplant, smoothing it out to cover the surface.

In a bowl, stir together myzithra, all but 2 tbsp of the gruyère, nutmeg, pepper, and salt to taste. Spread cheese mixture over meat layer. Sprinkle with remaining gruyère.

Broil moussaka 8 inches from heat for 8 to 10 minutes, until the topping is browned and the whole thing is bubbling. Let rest for 8 to 10 minutes to set before serving.

Serve garnished with chopped arugula and accompanied by a tomato or lettuce salad.

Serves 6

Soujoukakia Smyrna

Here are your basic meatballs in tomato sauce gone wild. With bold spicing, juicy sauce, and some potato and carrot as a bonus, this modest dish will even impress company.

½ cup dried bread crumbs

2 tbsp water

12 oz lean double-minced ground beef

12 oz lean double-minced ground pork

2 cloves garlic, finely chopped

½ cup finely diced onion

1 egg, lightly beaten

Salt and black pepper to taste

2 potatoes, cut in ¼-inch wedges

1 carrot, cut in ¼-inch sticks

4 cups tomatoes cut in ½-inch cubes

1 cup dry white wine

¼ cup olive oil

1 tsp ground cumin

1 tsp ground coriander

1 tsp dried chili flakes (optional)

Chopped fresh parsley, for garnish

In a bowl, stir together bread crumbs and water. Add ground meat, garlic, onion, egg, salt, and pepper. Shape mixture into 16 oval patties, and lay in one layer on a plate. Cover and set aside at room temperature for 30 minutes.

Heat 2 large frying pans on high heat for 3 minutes. Add potatoes and carrots to one pan and pan-dry, turning, for 10 to 12 minutes, until withered, browned, and tender.

Meanwhile, add tomatoes to second pan, sprinkle with salt to taste, and pan-dry, undisturbed, for 7 to 8 minutes, until saucy. Stir in wine, olive oil, cumin, coriander, optional chili flakes, and salt and pepper to taste. Transfer to a bowl and set aside.

Wipe pan dry and return it to high heat. Add meat patties and cook for 2 minutes, until browned on the bottom. Turn and cook other side for 2 minutes, until browned. Add tomato sauce and agitate pan to settle the sauce. Cook for 3 to 4 minutes for medium-rare (longer for well done), gently turning the patties in the sauce.

Arrange potatoes and carrots in the center of each plate. Spoon the patties and their sauce around them. Garnish with parsley and serve immediately.

Serves 4

Kefte

The meatball, if given even an inch, would conquer the world and never look back. Parent of the burger, and ground zero of inexpensive cuisine that'll please all members of the family at once, it deserves the attention of every cook. Here's a lovely meatball that satisfies without adding on the calories.

1 lb lean ground meat (preferably a
   combination of lamb, beef, and pork)
1 cup finely chopped onion
3 cloves garlic, finely chopped
1 cup dry bread crumbs, soaked in water
   and squeezed dry
1 egg, beaten
1 tbsp olive oil
1 tbsp dried chili flakes (optional)

Flavorings
1 tbsp ground cumin

OR
½ cup finely chopped mint
OR
2 tbsp dried oregano
OR
½ cup finely chopped fresh parsley

Chopped green onions, for garnish
Tzatziki (page 19) or plain yogurt
Pita bread (page 81)

In a large bowl, place ground meat, onion, garlic, bread crumbs, egg, olive oil, optional chili flakes, and flavoring of choice. Using your hands, knead until thoroughly mixed. Cover and refrigerate for 30 minutes to fuse flavors.

Shape mixture into meatballs 1 inch wide and ½ inch thick. Heat large frying pan on high heat for 3 minutes. Add meatballs and cook for 2 to 3 minutes per side, until crusted outside but moist inside (they will still be somewhat soft when pressed).

Garnish with green onions and serve immediately with tzatziki and pita bread.

Serves 4

Ouzo Sausage with Mushrooms

There is nothing mysterious or magic about making sausage. The casing can be tricky, but it is not needed when the sausage is made to order, as in this recipe. Regard this version as a template upon which to improvise your own variations. Look for a "sausage grind" of meat, a thicker texture than burger mince, for more substantial bite that sets this sausage apart.

1½ lb sausage-grind meat (12 oz each of any two of
 these: lamb, beef, or pork)
¼ cup ouzo
2 tbsp ground coriander
1 tbsp crushed anise seeds
½ tsp dried chili flakes (optional)
Salt and black pepper to taste
8 oz thinly sliced mixed mushrooms
 (such as button, oyster, and shiitake)

3 tbsp lemon juice
2 tbsp olive oil
4 semolina cakes (page 82)
Chopped fresh parsley and chives, for garnish
Tzatziki (page 19) or Lemon Mustard Sauce (see Box)
 for serving

In a large bowl, mix together well the ground meat, ouzo, coriander, anise, optional chili flakes, salt, and pepper. Shape mixture into 16 oval patties, and lay in one layer on a plate. Cover and set aside at room temperature for 30 minutes.

Heat 2 large frying pans on high heat for 3 minutes. Add mushrooms to one pan and pan-dry, turning once, for 4 to 5 minutes, until withered and somewhat charred. Add lemon juice, oil, and salt and pepper to taste. Cook, tossing, until liquid is absorbed, less than 1 minute. Remove from heat.

Meanwhile, add sausage patties to second pan and cook, turning occasionally, until browned all over, 4 to 5 minutes total for medium-rare (longer for medium and well done).

Place 1 semolina cake in the middle of each plate. Top with sausage patties and scatter mushrooms around the plate. Garnish with parsley and chives and serve immediately with Tzatziki or Lemon Mustard Sauce.

Serves 4

Lemon Mustard Sauce

2 tbsp Dijon Mustard
Juice of ½ lemon
2 tbsp olive oil
Salt and pepper to taste

Mix mustard, lemon juice, olive oil, and salt and pepper
to emulsify.

Rosemary Rabbit with Bulgur Kofta

Subsequent bites of the bulgur and rabbit make it hard to decide which is the better taste. Happily, these two marry each other seamlessly, and so the choice is easy: eat the two together.

Ask your butcher to bone a 3-lb rabbit. Unless you're a pro, it's difficult to do at home.

1 cup finely diced onion
1 cup raw bulgur (cracked wheat)
2 cups dry white wine (or half wine
    and half apple juice)
Salt and black pepper to taste
4 oz Cretan gruyère cheese, cut in ½-inch cubes
¼ cup chopped fresh parsley
2 tbsp toasted pine nuts
4 tbsp olive oil
1 lb 6 oz boneless rabbit, cut in ½-inch strips
    and medallions
1 cup mavrodaphne wine (or port)
4 sprigs fresh rosemary (or 2 tbsp dry)
Chopped green onion and finely diced tomato,
    for garnish

Heat deep pan on medium heat for 3 minutes. Add onion and cook, stirring occasionally, for 1 to 2 minutes, until softened. Add bulgur, wine, salt, and pepper. Cover and lightly boil for 12 minutes or until bulgur is tender. Stir in cheese, parsley, pine nuts, and 2 tbsp of the oil. Remove from heat, cover, and let rest for 1 hour, until cool.

Shape bulgur mixture into 4 round patties about ½ inch thick. Set aside.

Heat 2 large frying pans on high heat for 3 minutes. Add rabbit to one pan, sprinkle with salt to taste, and cook for 6 minutes, turning often to evenly brown all sides. Add mavrodaphne, rosemary, and black pepper to taste; cook for 3 to 4 minutes, until wine is somewhat reduced and saucy. Remove from heat and stir in remaining oil.

Meanwhile, add bulgur patties to second pan and cook for 2 to 3 minutes per side, until brown and slightly crispy on both sides.

Place a bulgur patty in the center of each plate. Spoon rabbit around bulgur, and drizzle pan juices over rabbit. Garnish bulgur with green onion and tomato and serve immediately.

Serves 4

Rabbit Stiffado

Stiffado is a combination of pearl onions, meat, and vinegar, plus attendant aromatics and spices. It is one of the highest-profile Greek specialties in the repertoire. It works with beef, but is at its best with rabbit.

Ask your butcher to bone a 3-lb rabbit.

1 lb pickling onions, peeled
8 cloves garlic, crushed
4 tbsp olive oil
2 tbsp demerara sugar
¼ cup red wine vinegar
¼ cup cider vinegar
1 lb 6 oz boneless rabbit, cut in ½-inch strips and
    medallions
Salt and black pepper to taste
1 cup semi-sweet red wine
2 bay leaves, halved
1 tbsp ground cinnamon
1 tsp grated nutmeg
5 whole cloves
2 cups tomatoes cut in ½-inch cubes

In a bowl, roll onions and garlic in 1 tbsp of the oil. Sprinkle with sugar and roll again to coat.

Heat 2 large frying pans on high heat for 3 minutes. Add sugared onions and garlic to one pan; cook, tossing, for about 5 minutes, until browned but not burned. Add red wine vinegar and cider vinegar; cook, shaking pan, for 1 to 2 minutes, until most of the liquid is absorbed.

Meanwhile, sprinkle rabbit with salt and pepper. Add rabbit to second pan and cook, turning occasionally, for about 5 minutes, until rabbit is browned on all sides and getting tender. Stir in wine, bay leaves, cinnamon, nutmeg, and cloves. Agitate pan over heat to mix for 1 minute.

Add tomatoes and the onions with their juices; stir well. Cook for 5 minutes, stirring a few times. Remove from heat and fold in remaining 3 tbsp oil.

Serve immediately with crusty bread.

Serves 4

Pork, Beef, and Poultry

Aristedes says:

The most important discoveries of my life have involved women. I have the hereditary Greek outlook that nothing in a man's life is of value unless it is done for the sake of a woman's happiness, or for a woman's pleasure, or at least was inspired by a woman. And so it happened with the creation of what I call my fruit cuisine, a refreshing voyage into the use of fruit with pork, beef, and poultry (as well as fish, seafood, and even pasta).

It was many years ago, during a hedonistic spell in Jamaica. The night was pregnant with the perfume of frangipani and datura. Reggae drifted up from the beach. And the exuberantly full moon, with the face of every woman I have ever loved, was poised on the "cheek of night" like forbidden desire.

I tried to sleep, but it didn't work. I looked out from the balcony, and there she still was, setting in the west, her sparkle dancing on the gentle surf toward me. I was at her mercy, I needed to do something to please her, to deserve her. So, I cooked for her. I had no kitchen in that hotel room, so I hallucinated dishes with which to enchant her. Without realizing what exactly I was doing, under that magical moon I invented all the basics of cooking with fruit. For her.

I conjured fragrant sauces; sweet-and-sour concoctions using fruits and fruit juices to accompany tender morsels of lightly cooked flesh; chutneys and relishes; compotes, preserves; and also raw fruit. I had been told that the seeds of the tropical soursop, prickly pear, and papaya are aphrodisiacs, naturally grown Viagra. In Greece, figs are believed to have the same effect, as are pomegranate seeds, with their juicy, blood-red mantle.

Which brings me to chicken. This most versatile of meats—just like its cousins, the duck and the goose—is a chef's best friend, because it allows for innovation and creativity without particularly offending expectation. We all know how to prepare chicken in at least ten ways. But in fact, there exist myriad ways. Chicken lends itself beautifully to being evoked with almost any fruit and herb combination imaginable.

Pork, beef, and poultry are the staples of meat eaters everywhere, and Greece, despite its leanings to lamb, goat, and rabbit, is no exception. It's just that we cook them tastier than everyone else.

Pork and Chickpeas Psiloritis

From the highest mountain of Crete comes a dish of substance to maintain fighting trim with which to survive in the forbidding terrain.

1 lb pork tenderloin, trimmed of fat and cut into
   1-inch-thick medallions
4 tbsp olive oil
1 tbsp finely chopped fresh sage
Salt and black pepper to taste
1 cup slivered yellow onion
4 cloves garlic, chopped
2 cups diced tomatoes
2 cups cooked chickpeas
1 tbsp dried thyme
3 tbsp chopped fresh parsley
½ cup dry white wine
Chopped fresh chives and plain yogurt (optional),
   for garnish

Brush pork with 1 tbsp of the oil. Rub with sage, salt, and pepper.

Heat 2 large frying pans on high heat for 3 minutes. Add onion, garlic, and salt and pepper to taste to one pan; cook, tossing, for 2 minutes. Add tomatoes and cook for 4 minutes, stirring occasionally. Stir in chickpeas and thyme and cook for 2 to 3 minutes, stirring, until saucy. Fold in remaining 3 tbsp oil and parsley. Remove from heat, cover, and let rest for about 4 minutes.

Meanwhile, add pork to second pan and cook, turning, for 4 minutes. Add wine, swirl the pan, and cook for 3 minutes for medium (2 additional minutes for well-done).

Mound chickpea-tomato stew in the center of each plate, and arrange pork over it. Garnish with chives and optional dollops of yogurt. Serve immediately.

Serves 4

Pork and Cabbage Siteia

Siteia is the forlorn belle, a last-ditch seductress awaiting her lover restlessly at the eastern edge of Crete, and this dish, with its pastel colors and sweet-sour tastes, matches her allure bite for bite.

1 lb green cabbage, cored and cut in
   1-inch-thick wedges
2 quince, peeled, cored, and cut in
   1-inch cubes (2 cups)
1 green apple, peeled, cored,
   and cut in 1-inch cubes (1 cup)
1 cup dry white wine
3 tbsp cider vinegar
Salt and black pepper to taste
4 tbsp olive oil
1 lb pork tenderloin, trimmed of fat
   and cut into 1-inch-thick medallions
1 tbsp dried marjoram
¼ cup calvados or other apple brandy
Chopped fresh chives, for garnish

In a deep pan on high heat, bring salted water to a boil. Add cabbage and quince; cook for 7 to 8 minutes, until tender. Drain, and return cabbage and quince to the pot. Add apple, wine, vinegar, salt, and pepper. Cook over high heat, stirring, for 2 to 3 minutes, until most of the liquid has been absorbed. Stir in 3 tbsp of the oil, remove from heat, and set aside.

Meanwhile, brush pork with 1 tbsp oil. Rub with marjoram and salt and pepper to taste. Heat large frying pan on high heat for 3 minutes. Add pork and cook, turning, for 4 to 5 minutes, until browned and cooked to medium (more for well done). Add calvados and cook, tossing, for 1 to 2 minutes, until absorbed.

Arrange beds of cabbage-quince mixture on plates and top with pork. Garnish with chives and serve immediately.

Serves 4

Pork and Mixed Peppers Yaourtlou

Tender pork greaselessly "breaded-fried," an array of flavors, and the sweet and creamy—but sinless—richness of yogurt: this is a mosaic of comfort food that always delights.

2 cups thinly sliced red bell pepper

¼ cup lemon juice

4 tbsp olive oil

Salt and pepper to taste

1 cup dry bread crumbs

2 cloves garlic

2 tbsp coriander seeds

1 tsp ground cumin

1 lb pork tenderloin, trimmed and cut into ¾-inch medallions

1 cup grated zucchini

½ cup chopped leek

½ cup plain yogurt

3 tbsp all-purpose flour

Sweet paprika (or cayenne, for spicy) and chopped fresh parsley, for garnish

In a small bowl, gently fold peppers with lemon juice, 3 tbsp of the oil, salt, and pepper. Let marinate for 15 to 30 minutes.

Blend together on high speed bread crumbs, garlic, coriander seeds, cumin, and salt and pepper to taste. Transfer mixture to a large bowl. Rub pork medallions with remaining 1 tbsp oil and add to the bowl. Toss pork until well coated with bread-crumb mixture.

Heat 2 large frying pans on medium heat for 3 minutes. Add coated pork and cook, turning occasionally, until golden brown, 8 to 9 minutes for medium, slightly more for well done.

Meanwhile, in a bowl, stir together zucchini, leek, ¼ cup of the yogurt, and salt and pepper to taste. Sift flour over mixture and stir to combine. Add this mixture to second pan in 4 dollops. Pat flat with a spatula and cook for 2 minutes or until beginning to brown on the bottom. Turn and cook other side for 2 minutes or until browned.

Place 1 pancake in center of each plate. Spoon a little of the remaining yogurt on the pancake and swirl some yogurt around the pancake. Arrange pork on the yogurt swirl. Arrange marinated peppers in between the medallions and on pancake. Sprinkle with paprika and parsley. Serve immediately.

Serves 4

Pork with Prunes and Almonds

Ancient Greek in concept, this partnering of browned meat with a sweet-and-sour sauce of fruit and nuts is a kind of heirloom taste that lingers in the pleasure centers of the mind and demands many encores.

1 cup blanched almonds
1 tsp ground cardamom
1 tsp ground allspice
Salt and black pepper to taste
4 pork tenderloins (1 to 1½ lb total), trimmed of fat
3 tbsp olive oil
1 cup dry white wine
5 tbsp plum jam
2 tbsp cider vinegar
8 pitted prunes, sliced lengthwise into quarters
4 cups steamed couscous
Chopped fresh chives, for garnish

Blend together on high speed almonds, cardamom, allspice, salt, and pepper until finely ground but still a bit gritty. Transfer mixture to a bowl. Rub tenderloins with 1 tbsp of the oil and roll them in almond mixture until well coated.

Heat large frying pan on medium heat for 3 minutes. Add coated tenderloins and cook, turning, until golden brown all over, 9 to 10 minutes for medium, slightly more for well done.

Meanwhile, blend together on high speed wine, jam, vinegar, remaining 2 tbsp oil, and salt and pepper to taste. Stir in prunes.

When pork is cooked, transfer to a warm plate, leaving behind in the pan the almond grits that fell off the meat during cooking. Return pan to high heat and immediately add jam mixture. Gently stir for 1 to 2 minutes, until sauce is slightly thickened. Remove from heat.

Quickly slice each tenderloin diagonally into 4 or 5 oval medallions. Fluff couscous by passing a fork through it several times. Mound couscous in the center of each plate. Spread a circle of sauce around the couscous and arrange pork over sauce. Garnish with chives and serve immediately.

Serves 4

Pork and Leeks on Celery-Lemon Custard

Subtle colors, delicate textures, and soothing but vibrant tastes underline the intense pleasures of a dish that is so simple to make it could grace a weekday, casual dinner, yet so elegant it could be the centerpiece of an elaborate celebration.

2 eggs
1 cup dry white wine
½ cup celery leaves
¼ cup lemon juice
¼ cup olive oil
1 tsp celery salt
¼ tsp black pepper
3 thin leeks, cut in 3-inch pieces
1 lb pork tenderloin, trimmed of fat and cut into
   ¾-inch medallions
Drained capers and chopped fresh chives,
   for garnish

Blend together on high speed eggs, wine, celery leaves, lemon juice, oil, celery salt, and pepper until custardy. Set aside.

Bring salted water to a boil in a deep pan. Add leeks and cook for 8 to 9 minutes, until tender. Drain leeks.

Meanwhile, heat large frying pan on high heat for 3 minutes. Add pork and cook, turning, until browned on both sides, 4 to 5 minutes for medium (more for well-done). Transfer pork to a plate and keep warm.

Reduce heat to medium. Add celery mixture and cook for 1 to 2 minutes, stirring constantly, until somewhat thickened (do not overcook or let boil, or it will curdle). Immediately remove from heat.

Spread a bed of custard on each plate. Arrange leeks in middle of each plate and surround with the pork. Garnish with capers and chives. Serve immediately.

Serves 4

Beef with Plum Mustard

The Chinese love sugar-coated sour plums. The French adore their mirabelle, or plum, tarts. The Yugoslavs swear by their plum slivovitz. And what would the English do without their "constitutional" prunes? It's unlikely that this plum-and-mustard concoction will take over entire nations, but it's enough if you and I know about it.

1½ cups thinly sliced pitted plums
1 cup mavrodaphne wine (or madeira or port)
¼ cup olive oil
2 tbsp chopped fresh tarragon (or 1 tbsp dried)
Salt and black pepper to taste
3 tbsp whole-grain or Dijon mustard
1 lb small new potatoes
20 pearl onions, peeled
1 lb boneless steak of choice, trimmed of fat
    and cut into 4 equal pieces
Chopped fresh tarragon or parsley, for garnish

Blend together on high speed half the plums, wine, oil, tarragon, salt, and pepper, until custardy. Fold in mustard. Set aside.

In a deep pan, cover potatoes with salted water. Bring to a boil over high heat and boil for 4 to 5 minutes, until tender. Drain, season, and keep warm.

Meanwhile, heat 2 large frying pans on high heat for 3 minutes. Add onions to one pan and cook, tossing, for 2 to 3 minutes, until browned. Add plum-mustard mixture and cook, stirring, until somewhat thickened, less than 2 minutes. Add remaining plums, stir for less than a minute, and remove from heat.

Meanwhile, add steaks to second pan and cook, turning to brown both sides, 2 minutes total for medium-rare, 3 minutes for medium, longer for well done. Time the cooking of the steaks to coincide with finishing the sauce.

Immediately spread a bed of sauce on each plate and top with a steak. Place potatoes on the sauce. Garnish with tarragon and serve immediately.

Serves 4

Hunkar Begendi

Beef on Eggplant Purée

The famous Ottoman concubine Hunkar, a notoriously hard-to-please gourmand, loved this combination, and it has been known as "Hunkar Liked It" ever since. Traditionally made with smoked eggplant purée mixed with tons of cream and butter, it is a lot lighter in this treatment of pan-dried smoked eggplant enriched with yogurt, and wonderful (if not quite as lean) when the optional cheese is used.

1 lb eggplant
½ tsp salt
4 oz shredded kasseri or cheddar cheese (optional)
3 tbsp thick plain yogurt
Salt and black pepper to taste
1 cup chopped fresh chives
½ cup puréed sun-dried tomatoes
¼ cup olive oil
3 tbsp water
1 tsp ground allspice
½ tsp ground cloves
1 lb boneless steak of choice, trimmed of fat
    and cut into 8 equal pieces
16 pickled baby onions (preferably in balsamic
    vinegar)

Peel eggplant and cut lengthwise into ¼-inch-thick sticks. Heat large frying pan on medium-high heat for 3 minutes. Add eggplant to pan, sprinkle with salt, and pan-dry, turning once, for 10 to 12 minutes, until withered, charred, and smoky. Transfer eggplant to blender. Add optional cheese, yogurt, salt, and pepper. Blend, pulsing, until mixed but still a little chunky. Fold in chives. Set aside.

In a small bowl, whisk together puréed tomatoes, oil, water, allspice, and cloves until smooth. Set aside.

Heat 2 large frying pans on high heat for 3 minutes. Add steaks to one pan and cook, turning to brown both sides, 2 minutes total for medium-rare, 3 minutes for medium, longer for well done.

Meanwhile, add eggplant mixture to second pan and cook, stirring, for 2 minutes, until warm and shiny.

Spread beds of eggplant purée on warmed plates. Place 2 steaks on each bed of eggplant. Spoon tomato sauce over eggplant and a little on the center of the steaks. Decorate with pickled onions and serve immediately.

Serves 4

Cypriot Beef and Yogurt

This dish, borrowed from Indian tandoori, has far less spice than its Asian parent but the same melting-textured meat. The wine-simmered potatoes are a distinctly European addition and make this a main-course dish instead of only a starter.

1 lb 6 oz boneless beef sirloin, cut into ¾-inch-thick
   medallions
1 cup plain yogurt
½ cup cold water
3 cloves garlic, mashed
1 tbsp dried oregano
1 lb small new potatoes
1 cup commandaria wine from Cyprus (or port)
¼ cup coarsely ground coriander seeds
Salt and black pepper to taste
4 tbsp olive oil
Coarsely chopped fresh coriander or parsley,
   for garnish

In a bowl, combine beef, yogurt, water, garlic, and oregano. Let marinate for 15 minutes at room temperature.

Heat 2 large frying pans on high heat for 3 minutes. Add potatoes to one pan and pan-dry, tossing, for 4 to 5 minutes, until golden all over. Stir in wine, coriander seeds, salt, and pepper. Reduce heat to medium, cover, and cook for 5 to 6 minutes, until potatoes are tender and have absorbed wine. Stir in 2 tbsp of the oil and remove from heat.

Meanwhile, using a slotted spoon, transfer beef, with as little liquid as possible, to the second pan (reserve marinade). Brown each side for 2 minutes for rare (longer for medium-rare and well done). Transfer beef to a plate and set aside, keeping warm. Immediately add to the pan the marinade and salt and pepper to taste; cook, stirring, until bubbling, and cook gently 5 minutes. Stir in remaining 2 tbsp of the oil and remove from heat.

Arrange beef in the middle of each plate. Drizzle sauce over the meat, and arrange potatoes around the beef. Garnish with fresh coriander and serve immediately.

Serves 4

Rosemary Chicken with Pistachios

This lively chicken dish, with sweet pistachios and the earthy flavor of rosemary, is perfect for a whiff of summer on a cold winter's eve.

This recipe also makes a wonderful pie filling: wrap inside oil-brushed pastry (thick filo, puff pastry, or homemade olive-oil crust) and bake at 350°F for 10 to 12 minutes until golden.

1 cup shelled natural pistachios
1 cup dry white wine
¼ cup olive oil
2 tbsp fresh rosemary leaves (or 1 tbsp dried)
4 large boneless skinless chicken breasts,
    cut into 1-inch nuggets
8 oz medium mushrooms, halved
Salt and black pepper to taste
3 tbsp strained yogurt (see page 12)
Chopped fresh chives and grated kefalotyri or
    romano cheese (optional), for garnish

Reserve 2 tbsp of the pistachios for garnish. Blend together on high speed the rest of the pistachios, wine, oil, and rosemary. Set aside.

Heat large frying pan on high heat for 3 minutes. Add chicken and cook, tossing, for 2 to 3 minutes or until brown all over. Add mushrooms, salt, and pepper; cook, tossing, for 2 minutes. Add pistachio mixture and cook, stirring, for 2 to 3 minutes, until chicken is cooked through but still springy to the touch. Remove from heat. Gently stir in yogurt to streak the sauce.

Garnish with reserved pistachios, chives, and optional cheese and serve immediately on rice, pasta, or potatoes.

Serves 4

Chicken Gruyère and Potato Pancakes

This chicken and potato stew benefits from the classic Greek flavorings of oregano, lemon juice, and olive oil, and is enriched with cheese that should preferably be the goat-and-sheep's milk gruyère of Crete.

1 cup dry white wine
1 tbsp dried oregano
3 tbsp lemon juice
2 tbsp prepared mustard of choice
Salt and pepper to taste
1 lb frying potatoes, cleaned
4 large skinless boneless chicken breasts or thighs,
    cut into 1-inch nuggets
4 oz Cretan or Swiss gruyère cheese, cut into
    ½-inch cubes
¼ cup olive oil
2 tbsp chopped fresh parsley
2 cups arugula or other bitter greens

Blend together on high speed wine, oregano, lemon juice, mustard, salt, and pepper. Set aside.

Grate potatoes and toss with salt to taste. Using your hands, squeeze out excess water. Divide potatoes into 4 equal portions and set aside.

Heat 2 large frying pans on medium heat for 3 minutes. Add 2 portions of potato to each pan, and flatten with a spatula into round cakes. Cook for 3 minutes or until browned on the bottom. Carefully flip and brown the other side for 2 to 3 minutes. Transfer potato pancakes to a warm platter and set aside, keeping warm.

Heat large frying pan on high heat for 3 minutes. Add chicken and cook, tossing, for 3 to 4 minutes, until evenly browned all over. Immediately add mustard mixture and cook, stirring, for 2 to 3 minutes, until chicken is cooked through but still springy to the touch and sauce is somewhat thickened. Add cheese, oil, and parsley. Fold and stir for 30 seconds. Remove from heat, cover, and let rest for 5 minutes.

Place 1 potato pancake on each plate and top with chicken and its sauce. Arrange arugula around the dish and serve immediately.

Serves 4

Chicken Yaourtlou

Yogurt, especially the sheep's milk version that is favored in Greece, enriches without adding many calories. Here it does its magic for chicken in an aromatic sauce.

2 tbsp sultana raisins
1 tbsp dried oregano
1 tbsp ground cumin
1 tbsp ground coriander
1 cup dry white wine
4 large skinless boneless chicken breasts,
   cut into 1-inch nuggets
2 cups thinly sliced leeks
4 cloves garlic, halved
3 cups diced tomatoes
Salt and pepper to taste
¼ cup olive oil
¾ cup plain yogurt
2½ cups cooked plain rice
Chopped fresh dillweed and toasted slivered
   almonds, for garnish

Stir raisins, oregano, cumin, and coriander into wine. Set aside.

Heat 2 large frying pans on high heat for 3 minutes. Add chicken to one pan and cook, tossing, for 3 to 4 minutes, until evenly browned all over.

Meanwhile, add leeks and garlic to second pan and pan-dry, tossing, for 2 to 3 minutes. Add tomatoes, wine mixture, salt, and pepper; cook, stirring, for 4 minutes or until saucy.

Immediately add browned chicken to sauce. Cook, stirring, for 2 to 3 minutes, until chicken is cooked through but still springy to the touch and sauce is somewhat thickened. Remove from heat and lightly fold in oil and ½ cup of the yogurt, leaving streaks of yogurt.

Mound rice in the center of each plate. Spoon chicken and sauce around rice. Put a dollop of the remaining yogurt on the rice. Garnish with dill and almonds and serve immediately.

Serves 4

Chicken with Eggplant

Eggplant is a vegetable that informs the Mediterranean kitchen more tellingly than any other ingredient. Here it is used with tender chicken and deeply aromatic coriander seeds.

8 cloves garlic, smashed
1 cup dry white wine
6 tbsp olive oil
3 tbsp lightly crushed coriander seeds
2 tbsp lemon juice
Salt and pepper to taste
1 lb eggplant
4 large skinless boneless chicken breasts,
    cut into 1-inch nuggets
Chopped fresh coriander or parsley, for garnish
4 homemade pitas (page 81)

Blend together on high speed garlic, wine, oil, coriander seeds, lemon juice, salt, and pepper until pasty. Set aside.

Cut eggplant into 1-inch cubes. Heat 2 large frying pans on high heat for 3 minutes. Add eggplant to one pan and cook for 4 minutes; turn and cook the opposite side for 2 minutes. Remove from heat.

Meanwhile, add chicken to second pan and cook, tossing, for 3 to 4 minutes, until evenly browned all over. Stir in wine mixture. Add eggplant and gently fold and cook for 2 to 3 minutes, until chicken is cooked through but still springy to the touch and most of the sauce is absorbed.

Garnish with fresh coriander and serve immediately heaped onto pita.

Serves 4

Chicken Saffron with Tangerine

The smoky flavor of the saffron and the sweet-tart taste of the tangerine transform this chicken into an exotic dish and an instant favorite, all at once.

1 cup dry white wine
1 cup tangerine or orange juice
2 tbsp sultana raisins
1 tsp saffron
4 large skinless boneless chicken breasts,
    cut into 1-inch nuggets
Salt and pepper to taste
¼ cup olive oil
4 large Politika Rice Croquettes (see Box)
Peeled tangerine segments and chopped fresh
    basil, for garnish

Combine wine, tangerine juice, raisins, and saffron. Set aside for 15 minutes.

Heat large frying pan on high heat for 3 minutes. Add chicken, sprinkle with salt and pepper, and cook, tossing, for 3 to 4 minutes, until evenly browned all over. Immediately add saffron mixture. Cook, stirring, for 3 to 4 minutes, until chicken is cooked through but still springy to the touch and sauce thickens somewhat. Stir in oil and remove from heat.

Serve immediately on rice croquettes, garnished with tangerine segments and basil.

Serves 4

Politika Rice Croquettes

2 cups boiled rice
½ cup chopped fresh herbs
½ cup finely chopped green onion
½ cup all-purpose flour
Salt and black pepper to taste
4 egg whites, beaten stiff
Melted butter (optional)

Combine rice, herbs, and green onion. Sift flour over mixture. Add salt and pepper; stir. Gently fold in egg whites.

Heat large frying pan on high heat for 3 minutes. Spoon 4 large dollops of mixture into pan, and, using wooden spoon, flatten into ovals. Cook 2 to 3 minutes, until bottom is crusted. Turn carefully and cook 2 to 3 minutes. You can slick the pan with melted butter to add delicious taste before you turn croquettes.

Chicken with Okra

Bamies, or okra, is present all over the sunbelt, from Louisiana to Crete to India. It thickens stews, it's full of nutrition, and it has a flavor that joins other sunbelt ingredients (like tomato and garlic) as if they were made for each other (they were). Here it partners chicken.

1 lb fresh or thawed frozen okra, trimmed

2 tbsp red wine vinegar

2 cups finely diced onion

4 cloves garlic, roughly chopped

3 cups tomatoes cut in ½-inch cubes

1 cup dry red wine

1 cup roughly chopped fresh parsley

¼ cup olive oil

1 tbsp dried chili flakes (optional)

Salt and black pepper to taste

4 large skinless boneless chicken breasts,
    cut into 1-inch nuggets

Toasted sliced almonds and chopped fresh mint
    and coriander, for garnish

Roll okra in vinegar. Set aside for 15 minutes.

Heat large frying pan on high heat for 3 minutes. Add onion and garlic; cook, stirring, for 2 to 3 minutes, until onion is transparent. Stir in 2 cups of the tomatoes, okra, and wine. Reduce heat to medium, cover, and cook for 7 minutes. Add the rest of the tomatoes, cover again, and cook for 3 to 4 minutes, until okra is tender. Remove from heat and stir in parsley, oil, optional chili flakes, salt, and pepper. Cover and let rest for 5 minutes.

Meanwhile, heat large frying pan on high heat for 3 minutes. Add chicken and cook, tossing, for 4 to 5 minutes, until evenly browned all over and cooked through.

Spoon a ring of okra on each plate. Mound chicken in the middle and top with almonds. Garnish with mint and coriander and serve immediately.

Serves 4

Kokoras Krassatos with Hylopites

Rooster in Wine with Pasta

This is the Greek recipe for rooster that gave birth to the French coq au vin. To prove it's Greek, it is traditionally served with egg-noodle bits that are known as hylopites (available in all Mediterranean markets). In a pinch you can use any short, flat pasta. And don't worry about finding rooster—any chicken will do.

4 large skinless boneless rooster or chicken legs
   and thighs, cut into 1-inch nuggets
8 cloves garlic, smashed
1 cup mavrodaphne wine (or port)
1 cup red wine
8 sprigs fresh rosemary (or 2 tbsp dried)
Salt and black pepper to taste
2 cups diced fresh tomatoes
4 oz Cretan or Swiss gruyère cheese, cut in
   ½-inch cubes
5 tbsp olive oil
10 oz hylopites pasta (or any short, flat pasta)
Chopped fresh parsley and grated kefalotyri or
   pecorino cheese, for garnish

Heat large frying pan on high heat for 3 minutes. Add chicken and garlic; cook, tossing, for 3 to 4 minutes, until lightly browned all over. Add mavrodaphne, red wine, rosemary, salt, and pepper; cook, stirring, for 1 minute. Add tomatoes; cook, stirring, for 2 minutes, until bubbly.

Reduce heat to medium, and cook, stirring occasionally, for 4 to 5 minutes, until saucy. Add gruyère and stir for less than 1 minute, until cheese is just beginning to melt but is still chunky. Remove from heat and stir in oil.

Meanwhile, cook pasta in boiling salted water until just tender, 6 to 8 minutes. Drain pasta.

Cover entire surface of each plate with pasta. Spoon chicken and sauce in the middle, leaving a wide ring of pasta around the chicken. Garnish pasta with generous sprinkles of parsley and kefalotyri.

Serves 4

Crispy Duck with Honey and Lemon

The most delicious part of the duck is its skin, but only if it's properly browned and crisped (so it's essential to follow the recipe to the letter). This is a dream recipe, with very little to do to make it perfect.

½ cup dry white wine
½ cup honey
¼ cup lemon juice
2 tbsp dried lavender flowers, chopped
2 tbsp lemon zest in thin ribbons
Salt and black pepper to taste
4 large boneless duck breasts (skin-on)
2 cups zucchini cut in ¼-inch rounds

1 cup hot or mild red banana peppers
   cut in ¼-inch-thick sticks
2 tbsp whole-grain mustard
¼ cup water
Salt and black pepper to taste
1 tbsp black and white sesame seeds
Sprigs of watercress, for garnish

Preheat broiler. In a small bowl, whisk together wine, honey, lemon juice, lavender flowers, lemon zest, salt, and pepper. Set aside.

Heat 2 large frying pans on high heat for 3 minutes. Add duck, skin side down, to one pan and sear for 4 to 5 minutes, until skin is brown but not burned. Tilt pan and spoon out as much fat as possible, discarding it. Turn duck and sear flesh side for 3 to 4 minutes, until browned but still pink inside (cook longer for well done).

Meanwhile, add zucchini and peppers to second pan. Pan-dry, tossing, for 4 to 5 minutes, until browned and tender. Stir together mustard and water and salt and pepper. Add to vegetables and toss to mix. Remove from heat and sprinkle with sesame seeds.

As soon as duck breasts are seared, transfer them, skin side up, to a broiler pan. Broil 6 inches from heat until skin is crisp, 2 to 3 minutes.

Meanwhile, add honey-lavender mixture to the duck pan (with leftover duck fat intact) and stir to deglaze. Cook, stirring, for 2 to 3 minutes, until syrupy. Remove from heat.

Spoon some sauce in the middle of each plate. Place the crisped duck on the sauce. Spoon vegetables around the duck. Garnish with watercress and serve immediately.

Serves 4

Crispy Duck with Apricots and Endives

Vegetables and duck with the enhancement of fruit and some sweet wine makes for very pleasant eating, especially if the duck skin has been properly crisped.

1 cup shelled natural pistachios, crushed
1 cup dried apricots, cut in ¼-inch thick strips
1½ cups limnos wine or Italian muscat
2 tbsp lemon juice
Salt and black pepper to taste
4 large boneless duck breasts (skin-on)
10 oz leeks, cut in 2-inch pieces
4 Belgian endives, cut in half lengthwise
¼ cup water
2 tbsp balsamic vinegar
Chopped fresh basil, for garnish

Preheat broiler. Blend half the pistachios, half the apricots, wine, lemon juice, salt, and pepper on high speed until smooth. Set aside.

Heat 2 large frying pans on high heat for 3 minutes. Add duck, skin side down, to one pan and sear for 4 to 5 minutes, until skin is brown but not burned. Tilt pan and spoon out as much fat as possible, discarding it. Turn duck and sear flesh side for 3 to 4 minutes, until browned but still pink inside (cook longer for well done).

Meanwhile, add leeks to second pan. Pan-dry, turning once, for 4 to 5 minutes. Add endives and continue pan-drying for 2 to 3 minutes, until vegetables are browned and tender. Add remaining pistachios and apricots, water, and vinegar. Toss gently for 1 minute to mix. Remove from heat.

As soon as duck breasts are seared, transfer them, skin side up, to a broiler pan. Broil 6 inches from heat until skin is crisp, 2 to 3 minutes.

Meanwhile, add pistachio-wine mixture to the duck pan (with leftover duck fat intact) and stir to deglaze. Cook, stirring, for 2 to 3 minutes, until syrupy. Remove from heat.

Spoon some sauce in the middle of each plate. Slice duck diagonally into 1-inch medallions, reshape breasts, and place on the sauce. Spoon vegetables around the duck. Garnish vegetables with basil and serve immediately.

Serves 4

Fish and Seafood

Aristedes says:

Greeks consider the creatures of the sea the ultimate luxuries of the table. Serve a Greek nicely turned out fish or seafood and you have a friend for life. I think it's a matter of our immense coastline: though small in surface area, Greece has 2,500 islands plus a craggy mainland with miles and miles of gentle seaside that allows for more active fishing villages to thrive here than in the rest of the Mediterranean put together. Every Greek lives within reach of the sea, which means a beach taverna with rickety tables, buttock-punishing chairs, and the day's catch, scintillatingly fresh fish and cephalopods and crustaceans and mollusks, simply cooked, doused in olive oil and lemon juice, to be eaten reverentially, accompanied by bottomless shots of ouzo or raki.

I tried the same formula in my eponymous restaurant on Toronto's Scollard Street, where I ruled Yorkville Greek-foodwise—maybe because mine was the only Greek restaurant in that high-rent district. It was a small place with a steadily uplifting atmosphere, mountains of seafood, rivers of ouzo, and as close to a beachy atmosphere as could be achieved 500 miles from the nearest salt water. The customers loved it, and so did I, thinking I had captured the feel of a restaurant in Crete's Ayia Galini or Psarou Beach in Mykonos.

And one day some visiting Greeks came for dinner. I think they were dignitaries, and they had heard just how Greek my place was. I made them comfortable, I loaded their plates with all manner of imported sea-delicacies—even sea urchin specially flown in from Chania—I cranked up the bouzouki music, I cracked open rare bottles of Greek wine and private-stock Cretan raki, I danced on their table, and at the end, they shook their heads, and they said "Nope"—or rather "Ochi"—"it's not the same as Greece."

This is not what a restaurateur wants to hear, not after he has bent over backwards. My disappointment must have been supremely obvious because they retreated slightly. "Okay"—or rather "Entaxi"—they said apologetically, "it was a great meal, but your fish was day-old." (Actually all "fresh" fish in Toronto comes from far away and is at least three days old.) "We prefer that it be from the same day. Your restaurant is commodious, but it's too nicely finished. We like things that are falling apart, as if they have been there for two hundred years. And you're not on the sea. We like to eat fish right at the edge of the water: it convinces us that the stuff is fresh and that you know what you're doing because your people and you have always lived by the sea and know fish."

I know perfectly what to do with fish, even if I haven't lived by the sea all my life. I have proven this to the Greeks in Greece, and I've proven it to non-Greeks everywhere else. But to those Greeks on that day in Toronto, I could prove nothing. I understand what they were getting at. It's that old cloying "magic" that was missing, a magic that can be realized only in the homeland.

Be that as it may, I always give my fish and seafood an extra little oomph, a gentle goosing, so that one can get the most out of them, especially since I am writing this book for people who live some distance from Greece. I have provided recipes for seafood I know to be available in North America and suggest alternatives if my original choice is difficult to find.

There are many fish and seafood recipes throughout this book. You will find them in the mezedes, they will be waiting for you in the salads, and also in the pasta and rice department. If it was up to the Greeks (and to me), fish and seafood would be served morning, noon, and night.

Fillets of Striped Bass with Citrus

Fish and citrus are a natural combination that is highlighted here by bitter greens and aromatic herbs.

½ cup blood orange, grapefruit, and/or
   orange juice
½ cup dry white wine
2 tbsp chopped fresh basil (or 1 tbsp dried)
1 tbsp lemon juice
1 tbsp mild mustard
Salt and black pepper to taste
1 tbsp drained capers
1 bunch chicory leaves or dandelions
8 striped bass or snapper fillets (about 1½ lb total)
¼ cup olive oil
1 tsp cornstarch dissolved in 1 tbsp water
Peeled grapefruit segments, and/or blood orange
   segments, and chopped fresh basil or parsley,
   for garnish

Blend together on medium speed citrus juice, wine, basil, lemon juice, mustard, salt, and pepper until emulsified. Stir in capers. Set aside.

Bring salted water to a boil in deep pan. Add chicory, cover, reduce heat to medium, and cook for about 5 minutes, until greens are tender and have lost some bitterness. Drain chicory, return to pan, and keep warm, covered.

Meanwhile, heat large frying pan on medium heat. Dry fish with paper towels. Add to pan, skin side down, and sear for 2 minutes. Turn and sear flesh side for 2 to 3 minutes, depending on thickness of fish. Transfer fish to a plate and keep warm.

Immediately add juice mixture to the pan. Cook for 2 to 3 minutes, until sauce has reduced by half. Stir in olive oil and cornstarch mixture and cook, stirring, for about 1 minute, until sauce just thickens. Remove from heat.

Arrange chicory in the center of each plate. Arrange fish around the greens. Pour spoonfuls of the sauce on the greens and the fish. Garnish with grapefruit segments and basil. Serve immediately.

Serves 4

Skate with Summer Vegetables and Capers

The delicious wing of the skate was mostly ignored in the past, save for the French, who have always enjoyed it poached and drowned in burnt butter. Here it is offered benignly dry-fried and dressed in a small amount of oil (and some optional butter). The fish will come in long pieces with easily managed, cartilaginous bones between layers of flesh.

1 cup dry white wine
2 tbsp olive oil
Salt and black pepper to taste
8 slices lemon, ¼ inch thick
8 oz carrots, cut in long ½-inch-thick pieces
8 oz zucchini, cut in long ½-inch-thick pieces
½ tsp salt

2 lb skinless skate, cut in 8 long slices
Salt and black pepper to taste
2 tbsp melted unsalted butter
½ cup drained capers, with ¼ cup caper brine
1 tsp cornstarch dissolved in 1 tbsp water
Chopped fresh coriander, for garnish

Whisk together wine, oil, salt, and pepper in a bowl. Set aside.

Lightly boil lemons in enough water to cover over medium heat for 10 to 12 minutes, until rind is soft. Drain and set aside.

Heat large frying pan on high heat for 3 minutes. Add carrots and pan-dry, tossing, for 2 to 3 minutes. Add zucchini, sprinkle with ½ tsp salt, and pan-dry, tossing, for another 6 to 8 minutes, until vegetables are tender, withered, and slightly charred.

Meanwhile, heat another large frying pan on high heat for 3 minutes. Dry the skate with paper towels. Season with salt and pepper. Add skate to pan and cook for 5 minutes. Turn and cook the second side for 5 minutes. Add butter and allow to brown; swirl pan for 30 seconds until butter is absorbed. Transfer skate to a plate and keep warm.

Add to the pan the wine mixture, lemon slices, capers, and caper brine; cook, swirling the pan, for 2 minutes. Add cornstarch mixture and stir for 30 seconds. Remove from heat.

Arrange vegetables in the center of each plate and place 2 skate pieces around the vegetables. Top skate with slices of lemon and sprinkle with coriander. Spoon sauce between pieces of skate and serve immediately.

Serves 4

Skate with Spinach, Olives, and Ginger

Poached skate is just as tender as the fried version in the previous recipe. Here it appears in tandem with licorice-flavored fennel and a sauce pungent with olive paste—refreshing in summer and nostalgically summery in winter.

1 bulb fennel, cut into ¼-inch dice
2 lb skinless skate, cut in 4 long slices
2 cups dry white wine
1 tbsp finely chopped fresh ginger
1 tbsp grated lemon zest
Salt and black pepper to taste
1½ lb spinach
1 cup thinly sliced leeks
3 tbsp green olive paste
½ cup chopped fresh chives
Chopped fennel leaves, for garnish

Preheat oven to 250°F. Heat large frying pan on medium heat for 3 minutes. Spread fennel in pan. Lay skate on top of fennel. Add wine, ginger, lemon zest, salt, and pepper. Cover and cook for 8 to 10 minutes, until fish is cooked through. Transfer skate to a baking sheet and cover with foil; keep warm in oven.

Meanwhile, heat large frying pan on high heat for 3 minutes. Add spinach, leeks, and salt to taste; cover and allow to steam in their own liquid for 5 minutes. Remove from heat and set aside until spinach is cool enough to handle. Working over a bowl to catch liquid, squeeze excess liquid from spinach, reserving spinach and liquid separately.

Add spinach liquid to fennel and pan juices. Cook for 5 to 6 minutes, until liquid has reduced by half. Remove from heat and stir in olive paste. Transfer sauce to blender and blend until smooth. Fold in chives.

Place a bed of spinach in center of each plate; place skate on spinach and spoon sauce around spinach. Garnish with fennel leaves and serve immediately.

Serves 4

Grouper with Green Beans

Grouper has delicious, full-bodied flesh that cooks sweet and melting. It has lots of its own flavor and can stand up to any enhancements, even if they are as assertive as the ones in this recipe. The olives required are the black, juicy, but withered sort that have an oily, soft texture. They often come from Morocco and Spain, but the ones from Greece are best.

1 cup dry white wine
¼ cup olive oil
1 tbsp dried oregano
1 tbsp dried marjoram
2 tbsp lemon juice
1 tbsp Dijon mustard
Salt and black pepper to taste
1 lb green beans, trimmed
4 grouper (or monkfish) steaks (each about 6 oz)
12 black olives, pitted and halved
8 sun-dried tomatoes, cut into thirds
¼ cup drained capers
1 tbsp lemon zest in thin ribbons
Chopped fresh parsley, for garnish

In a bowl, whisk together wine, oil, oregano, marjoram, lemon juice, mustard, salt, and pepper. Set aside.

Bring a deep pan of salted water to a boil. Heat large frying pan on high heat for 3 minutes.

Add green beans to boiling water and cook for 6 to 8 minutes (depending on thickness), until tender. Drain.

Meanwhile, dry grouper with paper towels. Add to frying pan and cook for 2 minutes. Turn and cook for 2 more minutes. Add wine mixture, olives, sun-dried tomatoes, capers, and lemon zest. Cook, gently turning grouper in the sauce, for 2 to 3 minutes, until fish begins to flake and sauce has thickened somewhat.

Place grouper in the middle of each plate. Arrange 2 stacks of green beans around the fish, and spoon sauce into the empty spaces. Garnish with parsley and serve immediately.

Serves 4

Mahi-Mahi with Pan-dried Tomato and Garlic

This dish is for fans of rich fishes permeated with beneficial fish oils, such as mahi-mahi and barracuda. A good fishmonger will gut, trim, and fillet fish for the price of a smile. The pan-dried tomato, with its freshness and retained moisture, will astound with its deep tomato flavor, which outshines that of sun-dried tomatoes.

1½ lb plum tomatoes, halved lengthwise
½ tsp salt
12 cloves garlic, smashed
8 mahi-mahi (or barracuda) steaks
   (each about 3 oz and ½ inch thick)
1 cup white wine
6 tbsp olive oil
½ cup chopped fresh basil
2½ cups cooked basmati or other long-grain rice

Heat 2 large frying pans on high heat for 3 minutes. Add tomatoes, cut side up, to one pan, sprinkle with salt, and pan-dry for 10 minutes, turning once, until withered and somewhat charred.

Meanwhile, add garlic to second pan and pan-dry, tossing, for 4 minutes, until lightly browned all over, without burning. Remove garlic from pan and set aside.

Dry mahi-mahi with paper towels and immediately add to second pan. Cook for 3 minutes, until well seared. Turn and cook for another 1 to 2 minutes, until lightly browned.

Meanwhile, add wine, oil, most of the basil, and browned garlic to the tomatoes. Cook, stirring, for 2 to 3 minutes, until saucy.

Mound rice on plates, and spoon sauce on two sides of the rice. Arrange mahi-mahi on the other two sides. Garnish with the rest of the basil and serve immediately.

Serves 4

Salt Cod Stew

Salt cod, a.k.a. bacalao, was probably invented by the Portuguese, but since the Greeks invented Portugal, Aristedes regards it as a thoroughly Greek product. The only challenge it presents is the soaking it must undergo to remove its salt and rehydrate its delicate flesh. Otherwise, it is easier to use than fresh fish, and absolutely delicious in a variety of dishes, including simple treatments like this stew. A bonus of this recipe is that the garlic sauce can be used with any other fish, with chicken, and even as a dip.

1 cup walnut bits

3 cloves garlic, smashed

6 tbsp olive oil

2 tbsp lemon juice

Salt and black pepper to taste

¼ cup water

1 lb salt cod, desalinated (see page 12) and cut into 4 portions

2 cups dry white wine

2 potatoes, cut in ¼-inch slices

1 small carrot, cut in ¼-inch-thick strips

2 zucchini, cut in ¼-inch rounds

2 thin leeks, cut in 1-inch pieces

16 Greek green olives, pitted and halved

2 cups tomatoes cut in ½-inch dice

1½ cups coarsely chopped celery leaves

½ cup red bell or banana pepper cut in ¼-inch rings

2 tbsp thinly sliced fresh chilies (or 1 tsp dried chili flakes)

2 tbsp sultana raisins

Coarsely chopped fresh parsley, for garnish

Blend together on medium speed walnut bits, garlic, 2 tbsp of the oil, lemon juice, salt, and pepper until smooth but still a little chunky. Add water and blend until smooth and lustrous. Set aside.

Heat large frying pan on medium-high heat for 3 minutes. Add cod, skin side down, and wine. Cover and cook for 8 minutes, until tender. Transfer cod to a plate and keep warm. Set aside the cooking wine.

Meanwhile, bring a deep pan of salted water to a boil over high heat. Add potatoes and carrots; cook for 5 minutes. Add zucchini and leeks; cook for 3 minutes. Drain vegetables and return to pan. Add reserved cooking wine, olives, tomatoes, celery leaves, red pepper, chilies, and raisins. Cook, stirring, for 3 to 4 minutes, until tomato is saucy but still slightly chunky. Remove from heat and stir in remaining 4 tbsp oil.

Spoon vegetables and sauce onto plates, place cod in the center, and top cod with a nice dollop of garlic-walnut sauce. Garnish with parsley and serve immediately.

Serves 4

Salt Cod with Saffron Potatoes and Beets

A greaseless "fried" salt cod on a bed of creamy, flavorful potatoes with a side of sweet oniony beets: pure bliss on any continent.

¼ cup dry white wine
2 tbsp lemon juice
1 tsp saffron
3 cloves garlic, smashed
3 tbsp olive oil
Salt and black pepper to taste
1 lb potatoes, peeled and cut in ½-inch slices
1 lb salt cod, desalinated (see page 12) and cut into
   4 portions
1 cup dry bread crumbs
Whole parsley, coriander, or basil leaves, for garnish
Beet and Onion Salad (page 49)

In a small bowl, combine wine, lemon juice, and saffron. Let infuse for 15 minutes. Transfer to blender and add garlic, 2 tbsp of the oil, salt, and pepper. Blend together on high speed until pasty. Set aside.

Boil potatoes in deep pan of salted water for 6 to 8 minutes, until tender. Drain, transfer to a large bowl, and add saffron mixture. Mash until smooth but still slightly lumpy. Set aside.

Meanwhile, heat large frying pan on medium-high heat for 3 minutes. Add cod, skin side down, and enough water to cover. Cover and cook for 8 minutes or until tender. Transfer cod to a plate. Peel off and discard skin.

Spread bread crumbs on a plate. Brush remaining 1 tbsp oil on both sides of cod and roll cod gently on bread crumbs to coat thoroughly and evenly.

Return frying pan to medium-high heat for 3 minutes. Add coated cod and cook each side for 2 minutes or until golden.

Spread beds of mashed potato on the center of large plates. Place cod in the middle of the potato. Garnish with parsley. Ring the plate with some Beet and Onion Salad, and drizzle a spoon or two of its dressing over it. Serve immediately.

Serves 4

Shark with Lemon-Dill and Asparagus

Shark does not have to mean Great White (which is quite likely delicious, except that Aristedes has not yet managed to catch one). Shark at fishmongers is a delicate, innocent-looking thing with textured, lean flesh and a clean flavor. Here it is presented with lemon-dill-garlic in a classic Greek recipe.

½ cup chopped fresh dillweed
½ cup dry white wine or water
5 tbsp olive oil
¼ cup lemon juice
4 cloves garlic, smashed
Salt and black pepper to taste
1¼ lb skinless boneless shark,
   cut in 1-inch medallions
16 spears asparagus

Add to blender ¼ cup of the dillweed, wine, oil, lemon juice, garlic, salt, and pepper. Pulse several times to blend until saucy. Set aside.

Heat large frying pan on high heat for 3 minutes. Dry shark with paper towels, season with salt and pepper to taste, and add to pan. Cook for 2 to 3 minutes to lightly brown one side. Turn and brown other side for 2 minutes.

Meanwhile, bring deep pan of salted water to a boil. Reduce heat to medium, add asparagus, and simmer for 3 to 4 minutes, until just tender.

Arrange 4 asparagus spears in the middle of each plate. Lean shark medallions on both sides of the asparagus. Drizzle lemon-dill sauce around fish and asparagus. Garnish with the rest of the dill and serve immediately.

Serves 4

Red Mullets Savoi

Red mullets (or barbounia) are the highest-prized fish in Greece, and they are usually simply fried and eaten with lemon. Aristedes prefers this zesty preparation to enliven an already alive flavor.

8 red mullets (2 lb total), scaled, finned,
   and gutted, heads on or off
¼ cup olive oil, plus extra for rubbing on fish
8 sprigs fresh rosemary
4 cloves garlic, chopped
¼ cup red wine vinegar
¼ cup cider vinegar
½ cup dry red wine
16 to 20 small new potatoes
Salt and black pepper to taste
Chopped fresh parsley and capers, for garnish

Preheat oven to 200°F. Heat large frying pan on medium for 3 minutes. Dry red mullets with paper towel. Rub the cavities with a little oil and place a sprig of rosemary and a portion of the garlic in each one. Add mullets to pan and cook for 4 to 5 minutes per side, until skin is browned and flesh lifts off the backbone when tested with a fork. Remove to a platter and keep warm in oven. Deglaze pan over high heat by adding vinegars and wine. Reduce liquid by about half. Add 3 tbsp oil, and salt and pepper. Reserve.

Meanwhile, in a deep pan, cover potatoes with salted water. Bring to a boil and boil for 4 to 5 minutes, until tender. Drain, return to the pan, add 1 tbsp olive oil, some chopped parsley, and salt and pepper, cover, and set aside.

Arrange mullets on warm plates. Arrange potatoes around mullets and drizzle mullets and potatoes with sauce. Garnish with parsley, capers and freshly ground black pepper and serve immediately.

Serves 4

Bonito Tuna with Mustard

Bonito is a petite tuna that has a stronger flavor than its huge cousin and a much more affordable price tag. It blends its flavors seamlessly with the aromatics and condiments of this recipe.

1 cup dry white wine or water
¼ cup Dijon mustard
1 tbsp dried oregano
3 tbsp lemon juice
Salt and black pepper to taste
4 bonito tuna (or mackerel) fillets (each 6 oz),
   cut in 4 equal pieces
1 cup leeks cut in ¼-inch rounds
1 lb Belgian endive cut in ½-inch rounds
2 tbsp honey
1 tbsp drained capers
1 cup grated daikon

Blend together on high speed ½ cup of the wine, mustard, oregano, lemon juice, salt, and pepper. Set aside.

Heat 2 large frying pans on high heat for 3 minutes. Add bonito to one pan, skin side down, and cook for 2 to 3 minutes, until browned. Flip and sear for about 1 minute, until flesh side is browned. Tuna will be rare. Cook for longer if you prefer well done.

Meanwhile, add leek and endive to second pan and cook, tossing, for 4 to 5 minutes, until somewhat browned and tender. Add honey and remaining ½ cup wine and cook, stirring, for 1 to 2 minutes, until liquid is absorbed.

Make a bed of leek and endive on each plate. Top with a piece of bonito. Nap bonito with mustard dressing. Sprinkle capers all over. Garnish with a hillock of grated daikon in the middle of the bonito and serve immediately.

Serves 4

Sardines with Red Peppers

Fresh European sardines are readily available on our shores and arrive in good condition, being oily fish and resilient to the long trek across the Atlantic. Gutting and scaling them is a bit of a challenge (most fishmongers refuse to get involved in the lengthy process), but it's worth it if for nothing else than getting to taste the real thing after years of the tinned.

2 cups red bell peppers cut in long
  ¼-inch-thick strips
1 cup green banana pepper cut in long
  ¼-inch-thick strips
¼ cup fresh chilies cut in long
  ¼-inch-thick strips
8 cloves garlic
1 cup fresh orange juice
3 tbsp lemon juice
4 tbsp olive oil
Salt and black pepper to taste
1½ lb fresh sardines, gutted and scaled
Chopped fresh coriander or chives, for garnish

Heat 2 large frying pans on high heat for 3 minutes. Add all three peppers to one pan and pan-dry, lightly tossing, for 4 minutes. Add garlic cloves and continue pan-drying and tossing for 3 to 4 minutes, until garlic is browned. Remove from heat.

Transfer garlic to blender. Add orange juice, lemon juice, 3 tbsp of the oil, a quarter of the mixed peppers, salt, and pepper. Blend until smooth; set aside.

Meanwhile, brush sardines with remaining 1 tbsp oil and add to second pan. Cook for 4 minutes to brown the bottom. Flip and cook the other side for 2 to 3 minutes, until flesh comes off the backbone at the touch of a fork.

Spoon remaining mixed peppers in the middle of the plates. Spoon sauce around peppers. Arrange sardines, browned side up, on the sauce. Garnish sardines with coriander and serve immediately.

Serves 4

Lemon-Garlic Prawns with Mushrooms

Prawns are everyone's favorite shellfish, and this recipe presents them in the simple but universally pleasing partnership of lemon and garlic. The mushrooms absorb most of the lemon, allowing the prawns' subtle flavor to shine through.

¼ cup lemon juice
¼ cup dry white wine
Salt and black pepper to taste
1 lb large prawns (about 16), peeled and deveined
12 cloves garlic, smashed
1 lb shiitake mushrooms (or button or oyster)
½ cup chopped fresh parsley, basil, or coriander
2 tbsp olive oil

Combine lemon juice, wine, salt, and pepper. Set aside.

Heat 2 large frying pans on high heat for 3 minutes. Simultaneously add the prawns and garlic to one pan and the mushrooms to the second pan. Cook, tossing contents of both pans, for 3 to 4 minutes, until mushrooms are browned and prawns are pink.

Add lemon juice mixture to mushrooms and toss for 1 minute, until mushrooms have absorbed liquid. Add mushrooms to the prawns, and swirl in parsley and oil. Toss for 30 seconds.

Serve immediately with crusty bread.

Serves 4

Prawns with Fennel and Ouzo

The triple licorice attack of fennel, ouzo, and dill provides a perfumed stage on which prawns perform their palate magic.

1 lb large prawns (about 16), peeled and deveined
1 lb fennel bulb, cut in ¼-inch thick slices
1 cup dry white wine
¼ cup olive oil
Salt and black pepper to taste
½ cup ouzo
¼ cup thick plain yogurt
Chopped fennel leaves or fresh dillweed,
   for garnish

Heat 2 large frying pans on high heat for 3 minutes. Simultaneously add the prawns to one pan and the fennel to the second pan. Cook, tossing contents of both pans, for 3 to 4 minutes, until fennel is browning and prawns are getting pink.

Add fennel to prawns. Add wine, oil, salt, and pepper. Cook, tossing, for less than 2 minutes, until all is saucy. Carefully add ouzo and stir for less than a minute (it might erupt in flames, which will subside as you stir). Add yogurt and stir very briefly.

Arrange fennel in a circle on plates with prawns in the center. Garnish with chopped fennel leaves and serve immediately.

Serves 4

Prawns Tourkolimano

Here is a lusty sauce of combined herbs, tomato, garlic, and feta, for the most Greek of all prawn recipes: a guaranteed crowd pleaser, as long as one remembers that feta is salty and to ease up on additional salt.

1 cup finely chopped green onion
6 cloves garlic, smashed
1 lb large prawns (about 16), peeled and deveined
4 cups finely diced tomatoes
1 cup dry white wine
1 tsp dried oregano
Salt and black pepper to taste
¼ cup each chopped fresh basil and mint
4 oz feta cheese, coarsely crumbled
¼ cup olive oil
Chopped fresh parsley and chives, for garnish

Heat 2 large frying pans on high heat for 3 minutes. Add green onions and garlic to one pan and pan-dry, tossing, for 2 to 3 minutes, until transparent.

Add prawns to second pan and cook, tossing, for 3 minutes, until springy.

Meanwhile, to the green onions add tomatoes, wine, oregano, salt, and pepper; cook, stirring occasionally, for 2 to 3 minutes, until saucy.

Add tomato mixture to the prawns along with basil and mint; cook, stirring, for 2 minutes. Gently fold feta and oil into the sauce. Remove from heat, cover, and let rest for 2 to 3 minutes.

Garnish with parsley and chives. Serve immediately with crusty bread.

Serves 4

Prawns and Artichokes with Sun-dried Tastes

Artichokes, a beloved resident of southern Europe. Olive-lemon-coriander, a North African flavor. Capers and sun-dried tomatoes from the islands, the stepping stones between the two coasts. Add prawns from the sea and you have a Mediterranean feast under any sky.

12 Greek or Italian green olives, pitted and roughly
   chopped
8 sun-dried tomatoes in oil, julienned
1 cup dry white wine
2 tbsp lemon zest in thin ribbons
4 tbsp olive oil
2 tbsp lemon juice
Salt and black pepper to taste
1 lb large prawns (about 16), peeled and deveined
12 cooked or canned baby artichokes
2 tbsp drained capers
2½ cups steamed plain couscous
Chopped fresh coriander or basil, for garnish

Blend together on high speed half the olives, half the sun-dried tomatoes, wine, half the lemon zest, 3 tbsp of the oil, lemon juice, salt, and pepper until pasty. Set aside.

Heat large frying pan on high heat for 3 minutes. Add prawns and cook, tossing, for 2 minutes or until they are getting pink. Add artichokes and cook, tossing, for 2 more minutes.

Add the capers, the tomato-olive mixture, and the rest of the olives, sun-dried tomatoes, and lemon zest. Cook, tossing, for 1 to 2 minutes, until saucy. Stir in remaining 1 tbsp oil. Remove from heat, cover, and let rest for 2 to 3 minutes.

Spoon a bed of couscous onto each plate and spoon prawns and sauce over and around it. Garnish with coriander and serve immediately.

Serves 4

Calamari Rethymno

Rethymno is the most charming town in Crete, and this charming recipe could become one of its favorites. It combines the best essences of squid, mushrooms, and pistachios for a quick and easy treat.

1 cup chopped fresh basil
   (or arugula or half of each)
½ cup shelled natural pistachios
1 cup dry white wine
6 tbsp olive oil
⅓ cup lemon juice
1 lb calamari bodies (tubes)
Salt and black pepper to taste
12 medium oyster mushrooms
Lettuce leaves

Blend together on high speed basil, most of the pistachios, wine, oil, and lemon juice until pasty. Set aside.

Slit the calamari bodies lengthwise, and open up into flat slabs. Dry with paper towels. Score flesh a few times with a sharp knife, without cutting through flesh. Sprinkle with salt and pepper.

Heat 2 large frying pans on high heat for 3 minutes. Add mushrooms to one pan and cook for 4 to 5 minutes, turning once, until browned on both sides.

Meanwhile, add calamari to second pan and cook, turning, for 3 to 4 minutes, until firm and starting to curl somewhat. Remove from pan and set aside. Add pistachio-basil sauce to the pan and cook, stirring, for 2 minutes. Remove from heat.

Arrange lettuce leaves on each plate. Arrange 3 mushrooms spoking out from the center. Place calamari in between the mushrooms. Drizzle sauce over the calamari, garnish with the rest of the pistachios, and serve immediately.

Serves 4

Lobster Santorini

Santorini is the magical rocky Aegean island that provides the definitive sunset view for Greek tourist posters. It is also the possible location of the legendary Atlantis, the current home of jet-setters and vacationing movie stars, and a place where splurging for dainty little lobster dishes is a daily ritual.

2 lb lobster tails
Salt and black pepper to taste
1 cup finely diced shallots
1 cup torn fresh basil leaves
1 cup vissanto wine from Santorini or sweet sherry
2 tbsp olive oil
1 tbsp lemon juice
4 cups cooked rice
Chopped fresh chives, for garnish

Shell and devein lobster tails, being careful not to split the meat. Cut tails into ½-inch-thick medallions. Sprinkle with salt and pepper.

Heat 2 large frying pans on high heat for 3 minutes. Add shallots to one pan and cook, stirring, for 1 to 2 minutes, until transparent. Add basil and wine; cook, agitating pan, for 2 to 3 minutes, until syrupy. Stir in oil and lemon juice and reduce heat to medium.

Meanwhile, add lobster to second pan in a single layer and cook for 1 minute. Turn carefully and cook for 1 minute more.

Add lobster to sauce and fold gently for 2 minutes. Remove from heat.

Mound rice in the middle of each plate. Spoon lobster and sauce around rice. Garnish rice with chives and serve immediately.

Serves 4

Ayion Oros on the Half Shell

Ayion Oros is a monastery complex that is most famous for forbidding members of the female sex—of any species—entry into its confines. Those who do get in (sorry, girls) may dine on delicacies such as this seafood stew, which on home base is harvested by the monks from the abundance of the sea coast down the hill from the monastery.

4½ lb mixed mollusks (mussels, cherrystone clams,
   round clams)
1 cup dry white wine
1 cup finely diced shallots
2 cups torn fresh sorrel leaves (or 1 cup chopped
   parsley mixed with 2 tbsp lemon juice)
2 tbsp mustard of choice
1 tbsp dried oregano
1 cup finely diced green or yellow banana peppers
¼ cup olive oil
Salt and black pepper to taste
8 raw oysters on the half shell
Grated daikon and chopped fresh chives,
   for garnish

Heat deep pan on high heat for 3 minutes. Add mollusks and wine. Cover and cook for 3 to 4 minutes, until mollusks have just opened. Place a strainer over a bowl and drain mollusks, reserving broth and mollusks in bowl. Discard any mollusks that did not open.

Return pan to high heat for 3 minutes. Add shallots and cook, stirring, for 1 to 2 minutes, until transparent. Add sorrel, mustard, oregano, and mollusk broth; cook, stirring, for 2 minutes. Stir in banana peppers, oil, salt, and pepper. Remove from heat and stir in mollusks. Cover and let rest for 5 minutes.

Portion mollusks into serving bowls. Arrange 2 oysters on the half shell on top of each portion. Garnish oysters with grated daikon, and garnish mollusks and sauce with chives. Serve immediately with crusty bread and lots of napkins.

Serves 4

Scallops and Asparagus on Linguine

The dual treat of scallops and asparagus enlivens this low-calorie, full-flavored pasta dish. And it's a visual delight if you're gentle with the scallops: the aim is to end up with lusciously browned scallop orbs as ornaments on a white and green hillock.

10 oz linguine
1 lb large scallops
Salt to taste
¼ cup metaxa or other brandy
2 tbsp unsalted butter, softened
1 lb asparagus, cut in 2-inch pieces
1 cup dry white wine
2 tbsp chopped fresh tarragon (or 1 tbsp dried)
2 tbsp olive oil
Black pepper to taste
Chopped fresh chives, for garnish

Cook linguine in boiling salted water until just tender, about 10 minutes.

Heat deep pan on high heat for 3 minutes. Add asparagus and reduce heat to medium. Pan-dry asparagus, tossing, for 3 to 4 minutes (longer if thick), until just tender. Add wine, tarragon, oil, salt to taste, and pepper. Cook, stirring, for 1 minute.

Working quickly, drain linguine and add to asparagus. Toss and fold to mix well. Remove from heat.

Meanwhile, heat large frying pan on high heat for 3 minutes. Dry scallops with paper towels and add to pan; sprinkle with salt. Sear for 1 minute. Turn delicately and sear other side for 1 minute. Carefully add brandy (it might erupt in flames) and butter; let sizzle for 1 to 2 minutes, agitating pan to distribute glaze to all the scallops. Scallops should be brown on one side. Set aside.

Divide linguine and asparagus among plates. Arrange scallops, browned side up, on linguine. Garnish with chives and serve immediately.

Serves 4

Vegetables and Legumes

Aristedes says:

A famous Greek poet and Nobel laureat, Odysseas Elytis, in his epic poem, *Axion Esti*, begins appropriately with a chapter entitled "Genesis" in which he divines the birth of the world.

According to Elytis, God created Earth when still fairly young and inexperienced. I imagine that, therefore, He worked hard, and He shaped and built everything to His youthful satisfaction, but He was left with a great heap of rocks. He collected them, because they were unsightly, and He flung them over His shoulder. When He turned to see how they had landed, He was faced with a hilly, jagged spectacle, which He called Hellas.

I extrapolate further that a young God would be unhappy with the dry, unfriendly terrain. He therefore softened the rocks with a border of multi-blue sea, and He blessed the arid hills to grow whatever plants they could.

But God also gave Greece the Greeks, who then proceeded to cultivate wherever they could find fertile soil, and thus were born our vegetables and legumes and olives and fruits: the staples of our diet. Greeks adore fish, and they will always enjoy red meat and chicken, but they are foremost vegetarians. Flesh is luxury, but beans and grains and vegetables are necessities. And like any resourceful nation, Greece too has employed invention to mother its necessities.

Drawing on a long history of outside influences, Greeks have evolved a meatless repertoire to rival even India's, the globe's most articulated vegetarian culture.

Many of our best vegetarian dishes are soups, salads, and pasta or rice dishes. There are, however, significant main-course items, which you will find in this section. I love all of them, but I'm a particular fan of arti-chokes cooked Constantinopolitan style, which you will find listed as Artichokes . . . la Polita.

During an interminable flight from Constantinople to Quito, via Amsterdam, Miami, and Mexico City, thirty hours in economy class and its repetitively inedible meals, I survived solely on a fortuitous preflight take-out of copious quantities of said artichokes from a small restaurant in the ancient Byzantine capital. When I finally arrived in Ecuador, with all of Central American cuisine at my disposal, all I really craved was more artichokes.

Being the insatiable omnivore that I am, I also craved briami (Greek ratatouille) and imam bayildi (eggplant with tomato and currants) and fassolia plaki (Greek stewed beans) and all the other vegetable classics with which I grew up. Except that they were impossible to cook in the Quito hotel where I was staying, and there was a curious paucity of Greek restaurants in the Ecuadorian capital—a failing that must be addressed, since there are Greek restaurants everywhere else in the world.

Happily, you won't have to crave them without satisfying yourself, because here you will find specially adapted recipes for all of the above. And more good news: my recipes for these dishes cook up in less than half hour, preparation time included.

Summer Garden Vegetables

A short while ago Greeks discovered that vegetables are edible even when they aren't obliterated by over-boiling. These days, gently boiled vegetables are appearing on a lot of tables as both salad and side dish. It could be claimed that Greeks are finally eating their vegetables, and enjoying them too—even more so when they dress them up Aristedes-style, as here.

2 cups potatoes cut in ½-inch cubes
6 cups mixed vegetables of choice (broccoli,
　green beans, cauliflower, zucchini, rapini, etc.)
　cut in bite-sized pieces
¼ cup chopped fresh basil
¼ cup dry white wine
¼ cup olive oil
2 tbsp Dijon mustard
2 tbsp white wine vinegar
¼ cup chopped pitted Greek black olives
¼ cup sun-dried tomatoes in oil, chopped
2 tbsp drained capers
8 anchovies, very finely chopped
Freshly ground black pepper and strips of
　red bell pepper, for garnish
Hard boiled eggs, cut in quarters, for garnish
　(optional)

Cook potatoes in boiling salted water until tender. Drain and set aside.

Steam or boil mixed vegetables to desired tenderness (about 5 minutes for crisp-tender, longer for softer). Drain.

Meanwhile, in a large bowl, whisk together basil, wine, oil, mustard, and vinegar until lightly emulsified. Stir in olives, sun-dried tomatoes, capers, and anchovies. Stir to mix well. Add potatoes and mixed vegetables; fold to mix well.

Divide mixture among plates. Garnish with black pepper, red pepper strips, and optional eggs, and serve immediately while still warm.

Serves 4 to 6

Artichokes à La Polita

Constantinople and its multi-millennial Hellenism is the origin of many Greek recipes, many of the best of which are vegetarian, as is this one.

½ cup grapefruit juice
¼ cup olive oil
2 tbsp chopped fresh dillweed
2 tbsp lemon juice
Salt and pepper to taste
1 lb potatoes, peeled and cut in 1-inch cubes
8 oz carrots, cut in ½-inch rounds
8 pickling onions (1 inch diameter)
1 cup fresh or frozen green peas
12 boiled fresh baby artichokes
½ cup plain yogurt
4 oz feta cheese
Sprigs of fresh dillweed and peeled grapefruit
    segments, for garnish

Whisk together grapefruit juice, oil, dill, lemon juice, salt, and pepper until emulsified. Set aside.

Bring salted water to a boil in a deep pan. Add potatoes, carrots, and onions; cook for 8 to 10 minutes, until tender. Add peas and artichokes; cook for 1 minute. Drain vegetables and transfer to a salad bowl. Add the grapefruit dressing and toss gently to coat vegetables. Salad can be served warm or within 2 hours, at room temperature.

When ready to serve, arrange salad on plates. Blend together yogurt and feta on high speed. Add a dollop of yogurt-feta sauce to salad; distribute grapefruit segments and garnish with dill.

Serves 4

Imam Bayildi

Eggplant with Tomato and Currants

Normally this dish is meant to be drowning in oil (the exorbitant excess of which makes the "imam faint," as the translation of the Turkish title testifies). Aristedes' "hot pan, no oil" method uses a small amount of oil and produces a textured eggplant that retains its flavor the way the mushy original never could.

1 lb eggplant
Salt to taste
1 cup thinly sliced onion
6 cloves garlic, chopped
2 cups diced tomatoes
½ cup dry white wine
3 tbsp currants
2 tbsp chopped fresh mint
Black pepper to taste
2 tbsp chopped fresh parsley
¼ cup olive oil
½ cup chopped fresh chives
Browned pine nuts and coarsely crumbled
   feta cheese (optional), for garnish

Heat 2 large frying pans on high heat for 3 minutes. Cut eggplant into 1-inch cubes. Add eggplant to one pan, making sure all the pieces touch the hot surface, and sprinkle with salt. Cook, turning occasionally, for 6 to 8 minutes, until golden brown all over and tender.

Meanwhile, add onion and garlic to second pan. Cook for 2 to 3 minutes, until onion is transparent. Add tomatoes, wine, currants, mint, salt to taste, and pepper. Cook, stirring, for 3 to 4 minutes, until saucy. Add parsley and eggplant; gently fold into the sauce for 3 or 4 minutes. Remove from heat, fold in oil, cover, and let rest for 5 minutes.

Sprinkle chives on plates. Spoon eggplant over the chives. Garnish with pine nuts and optional feta and serve immediately or at room temperature up 2 hours later as a salad.

Serves 4

Briami

Greek Ratatouille

Most recipes for this, the Mediterranean's favorite combination, call for vegetables and loads of garlic baked in a pool of oil. This version uses neither garlic nor excessive oil, highlighting the natural flavors and clean textures of the vegetables themselves.

1½ lb ripe tomatoes, coarsely chopped
¼ cup olive oil
2 tbsp each chopped fresh parsley, mint, and basil
Freshly ground black pepper to taste
8 oz eggplant
1 lb potatoes, cut in 1-inch cubes
8 oz carrots, in long ½-inch-thick pieces
½ tsp salt
1 cup thinly sliced red bell pepper
8 oz zucchini, cut in long ½-inch-thick pieces
6 oz sliced Cretan or Swiss gruyère cheese
Arugula or other bitter leaves

Blend together, pulsing to achieve a chunky sauce, tomatoes, oil, parsley, mint, basil, and black pepper. Set aside.

Peel eggplant and cut lengthwise into ¼-inch-thick strips. Heat 1 large frying pan and 1 deep pan on high heat for 3 minutes. Add potatoes and carrots to deep pan, sprinkle with ½ tsp salt, and pan-dry, turning, for 6 to 7 minutes. Add bell pepper and continue to pan-dry for another 5 to 6 minutes, until everything is tender, withered, and slightly charred.

Simultaneously, add eggplant to frying pan, sprinkle with salt to taste, and pan-dry for 4 minutes. Add zucchini and continue to pan-dry, turning once, for another 6 to 7 minutes, until everything is tender, withered, and slightly charred.

Add contents of frying pan to deep pan, reduce heat to low, and add tomato sauce. Turn vegetables in the sauce to coat, and smooth out to cover the bottom of the pan. Top with cheese. Cover and cook, undisturbed, for less than 3 minutes, until cheese is melted.

Scoop a quarter of the briami, with cheese on top, onto each plate and circle with arugula leaves. Garnish with black pepper and serve immediately.

Serves 4

Mushrooms Mykonos

Mykonos is the most popular Greek island with both tourists and locals, and for good reason. It is beautiful, it has the best swimming in the Mediterranean, and it endears itself with an addictively insouciant lifestyle. Its restaurants go with the flow, with delicious and simple fare like these mushrooms.

5 cloves garlic, roughly chopped
¼ cup olive oil
¼ cup grapefruit juice
1 tbsp dried oregano
3 tbsp lemon juice
1 tsp black pepper
1 lb 6 oz mixed mushrooms (such as button,
    oyster, and shiitake), cut in large pieces
Salt to taste
½ cup chopped fresh parsley
Watercress, arugula, or other bitter leaves

Blend together on high speed garlic, oil, grapefruit juice, oregano, lemon juice, and pepper until pasty. Set aside.

Heat large frying pan on high heat for 3 minutes. Add mushrooms, sprinkle with salt, and pan-dry, turning, for 5 to 6 minutes, until withered, browned, and slightly charred. Remove and reserve, warm.

Add grapefruit dressing to pan; simmer for 1 to 2 minutes to reduce by about one-third. Remove from heat and stir in parsley.

Spoon mushrooms in the middle of each plate. Surround with watercress. Pour sauce over and serve immediately.

Serves 4

Green Beans with Lavender Croutons

These are the traditional green beans of Greece, which have been modified by Aristedes. They are cooked to the point (instead of to death), and they are accessorized by the unusual, but highly complementary, perfume of lavender. They make for a light supper (with steamed rice) or an excellent side course for lamb or beef.

6 tbsp olive oil
¼ cup chopped fresh lavender blossoms
   (or 2 tbsp chopped fresh marjoram)
Salt and black pepper to taste
8 oz onions, finely sliced
8 cloves garlic, roughly chopped
4 cups tomatoes cut in ½-inch cubes
1 lb green beans, trimmed and halved diagonally
1 lb potatoes, cut in ½-inch cubes
4 oz black olives, pitted
1 cup coarsely chopped fresh parsley
2 cups homemade plain croutons
8 oz feta cheese, coarsely crumbled

In a large bowl, stir together 2 tbsp of the oil, lavender, salt, and pepper. Set aside.

Heat deep pan on high heat for 3 minutes. Add onions and garlic; cook, tossing, for 2 to 3 minutes, until onions are transparent. Add tomatoes, green beans, and potatoes. Reduce heat to medium and cover. Cook, stirring once or twice, for 10 to 12 minutes, until vegetables are tender. Add olives, remaining 4 tbsp oil, and salt and pepper to taste. Cook for 2 minutes, stirring once. Remove from heat and fold in parsley. Cover and let rest for 10 minutes.

Add croutons to lavender oil; toss to mix well. Arrange beans on plates, surround with croutons, and top with feta. Serve immediately.

Serves 4 as a main course, 6 to 8 as a starter or side dish

Zucchini-Chestnut Stiffado

This is a stiffado for those who can't face eating rabbit but still want to enjoy the thrill of vinegared-sweetened onions highlighting an aromatic stew (in this case one of zucchini and chestnuts). Add crusty bread and a glass of rosé, and this little dish could become your favorite lunch.

If fresh chestnuts aren't available, you can use the bottled roasted ones.

1 lb pickling onions, peeled
5 cloves garlic, smashed
2 tbsp granulated sugar
4 tbsp olive oil
¼ cup red wine vinegar
1 lb 6 oz zucchini, cut in long ½-inch-thick strips
Salt to taste
8 oz chestnuts, boiled, peeled, and skinned
1 cup semi-sweet red wine
½ cup water
2 tbsp lemon juice
1 tsp ground cloves
2 bay leaves, halved
Black pepper, to taste
Slices of prickly pear and pomegranate seeds,
   for garnish

In a bowl, roll onions and garlic in sugar and 1 tbsp of the oil to coat. Heat 2 large frying pans on high heat for 3 minutes. Add sugared onions and garlic to one pan; cook, tossing, for about 5 minutes, until browned but not burned. Add vinegar; shake pan for 1 to 2 minutes, until vinegar is absorbed.

Meanwhile, add zucchini to second pan, sprinkle with salt, and pan-dry, tossing, for 6 to 8 minutes, until browned and tender.

To the onions add chestnuts, wine, water, lemon juice, cloves, bay leaves, salt to taste, and pepper. Cook, turning, for about 5 minutes, until saucy. Remove from heat and fold in remaining 3 tbsp oil.

Arrange zucchini in the middle of each plate. Spoon onions and sauce around zucchini. Garnish with prickly pear and pomegranate and serve immediately.

Serves 4

Vegetarian Moussaka

Moussaka normally evokes visions of greasy meat, even greasier eggplant, and an unbearably fatty béchamel topping. We all love it anyway, but you'll no doubt prefer Aristedes' light versions, either with meat (see page 96) or meatless, as here. Because all moussakas are somewhat labor-intensive, this is a larger recipe suitable for entertaining.

If fresh chestnuts aren't available, you can use the bottled roasted ones.

12 oz chestnuts, boiled, peeled, and skinned

2 cups thick yogurt

1 cup shredded Cretan or Swiss gruyère cheese

1 tsp dried chili flakes (optional)

Salt and black pepper to taste

1 lb eggplant

1 lb zucchini, cut in long ¼-inch-thick strips

2 cups thinly sliced onion

6 cloves garlic, slivered

5 cups tomatoes cut in ½-inch cubes

2 tbsp chopped fresh sage (or 1 tbsp dried)

2 tbsp chopped fresh marjoram (or 1 tbsp dried)

2 cups cooked lentils (or chickpeas, or half of each)

3 tbsp currants

5 tbsp olive oil

Chopped fresh parsley, for garnish

In a bowl, mash chestnuts, yogurt, ¾ cup of the cheese, optional chili flakes, and salt and pepper until smooth. Set aside.

Peel eggplant and cut lengthwise into long ¼-inch-thick strips. Heat 2 large frying pans on high heat for 3 minutes. Add eggplant to one pan, sprinkle with salt, and pan-dry, turning once, for 8 to 10 minutes, until tender, withered, and somewhat charred.

Meanwhile, add zucchini to second pan and pan-dry, turning once, for 6 to 8 minutes, until tender, withered, and somewhat charred.

Arrange eggplant in a nonstick baking dish; top with zucchini. Set aside.

Preheat broiler. Heat one of the frying pans on high heat for 3 minutes. Add onion and garlic; cook, tossing, for 2 to 3 minutes, until onion is softened. Add tomatoes, sage, marjoram, salt and pepper to taste; cook, stirring, for about 3 minutes, until thickened. Add lentils and currants; cook, stirring, for 2 minutes. Remove from heat and stir in oil.

Spread tomato-lentil mixture over zucchini and eggplant. Spread chestnut mixture over that, and sprinkle with remaining ¼ cup cheese. Broil moussaka 8 inches from heat for 3 to 4 minutes, until cheese is bubbling and beginning to brown.

Portion onto plates, garnish with parsley, and serve immediately.

Serves 6

Lentil-Chickpea Pancake Salad

A protein-pack of tastes and textures with a perky sauce, this is comfort vegetarian fare that will brighten (and fortify) even the stormiest day of winter.

6 anchovy fillets
4 cloves garlic, roughly chopped
½ cup sunflower or pumpkin seeds
½ cup grapefruit juice
5 tbsp olive oil
Salt and black pepper to taste
1½ cups cooked lentils
1 cup cooked chickpeas
¾ cup chickpea flour
¼ cup plain yogurt
2 cups bitter salad leaves
1 cup tomato cut in ½-inch cubes
½ cup chopped green onion
3 tbsp lemon juice
Chopped fresh parsley, for garnish

Blend together on high speed anchovies, garlic, sunflower seeds, grapefruit juice, 3 tbsp of the oil, salt, and pepper until pasty. Set aside.

In a bowl, combine lentils, chickpeas, chickpea flour, yogurt, and salt and pepper to taste. Stir until the mixture is sticky. Shape mixture into four ½-inch-thick pancakes.

Heat large frying pan on medium heat for 3 minutes. Add pancakes and cook for 4 minutes or until brown on the bottom. Flip and brown second side for about 4 minutes.

Meanwhile, combine bitter salad leaves, tomato, and green onion in a large bowl. Sprinkle with lemon juice and remaining 2 tbsp oil; toss to coat.

Place a pancake in the middle of each plate. Surround with salad. Top each pancake with a dollop of anchovy sauce. Garnish with parsley and serve immediately.

Serves 4

Mavromatika

Black-eyed Pea Salad

As legumes go, the black-eyed pea is special to a number of sunbelt, bean-eating cultures around the globe. The Greeks eat them (and lentils) to bring joy to fasts, such as the forty-day Lenten abstention from meat. Full of protein and taste, this is a recipe for a lovely meatless meal any time of year. Alternatively, serve with smoked mackerel, smoked trout, or smoked sturgeon and Lemon Mustard Sauce (page 99).

½ cup grapefruit juice
¼ cup olive oil
1 tbsp chopped fresh rosemary (or 1 tsp dried)
2 tbsp cider vinegar
2 tbsp white wine vinegar
2 cloves garlic, chopped
Salt and black pepper to taste
4 cups cooked black-eyed peas
1 cup tomato cut in ½-inch cubes
½ cup grated carrot
¼ cup finely chopped celery
¼ cup chopped green onion
¼ cup cucumber cut in ¼-inch dice
¼ cup red bell pepper cut in ¼-inch dice
Chopped fresh parsley, for garnish

Blend together on high speed grapefruit juice, oil, rosemary, cider vinegar, wine vinegar, garlic, salt, and pepper until emulsified.

In a large bowl, combine black-eyed peas, tomato, carrot, celery, green onion, cucumber, and red bell pepper. Add grapefruit dressing and toss gently to dress and mix the ingredients.

Garnish with parsley and serve within 2 hours.

Serves 6

Fassolia Plaki

Greek Stewed Beans

Every culture on the planet has a favorite bean stew, be it the frijoles negros of Cuba or the molasses-drenched fèves au lard of Quebec. This recipe is for Greek-style beans, complete with all of the home country's favored condiments.

2 cups thinly sliced leeks (or 1 cup diced onion)
6 cloves garlic, roughly chopped
2 cups cooked romano beans
½ cup boiling water
2 cups dry red wine
¼ cup currants
¼ cup black olive paste
1 tbsp dried thyme or savory
10 sun-dried tomatoes, chopped in thirds
2 tbsp drained capers
2 tbsp olive oil
1 tsp black pepper
Toasted sunflower and/or pumpkin seeds and
   chopped green onion, for garnish

Heat deep pan on high heat for 3 minutes. Add leek and garlic; cook, stirring, for 2 to 3 minutes, until leek is transparent. Fold in beans and water. Add wine, currants, olive paste, and thyme; cook, stirring, for 6 minutes. Add sun-dried tomatoes, reduce heat to medium, and cook, stirring gently, for 3 to 4 minutes, until saucy. Stir in capers, oil, and pepper. Remove from heat, cover, and let rest for 5 minutes.

Spoon beans onto plates. Garnish with seeds and green onion and serve immediately.

Serves 4

Desserts

Aristedes says:

I view all of life as dessert. To call me a sweets junkie is no exaggeration. I've been known to eat desserts as a starting course, and even instead of dinner. And I've dedicated a good part of my time in the kitchen to baking, icing, glazing, and making sweets and post-prandial delicacies.

One of the many family legends about me is that I baked my first cake when I was four. I loved watching my mother make her cakes, and naturally, like any child, I loved licking out the mixing bowl. On a particular cake-making day, my mother had all her ingredients out when she was called away, leaving me alone in the kitchen.

I took over, making a giant mess—something that I am still guilty of when I cook or bake—but managed to put in the right things and even turned on the oven and put my cake in there. My mother returned to a sweet aroma in the house, and was faced with a rising, almost golden cake when she opened the oven door. Her gasp of sheer surprise still sends goose pimples down my back. They tell me that my maiden cake turned out just fine and was devoured in one sitting.

Greek desserts have gotten bad press just because they have been known to drip with sickly-sweet syrups. Well, okay. But that can be contained, as you will see in this section. Otherwise, Greek desserts, some of which are from ancient Byzantium, some from Italy, many from the Middle East (via the Ottomans), are a carnival of fruit and nuts and sweet spices, and feather-light crusts buttered to meltingness. In every way, the perfect way to end a meal of Greek flavors done the Aristedes way.

In the pages that follow, I offer you everything you'll need to feel Greek at dessert time. From the inevitable baklava—in three versions just to be safe—to my world-famous bougatsa, here enhanced with apples, though any solid-fleshed fruit will do or, even better, a combination of fruits. There is also a soufflé-like walnut karithopita that could well redefine that neglected nut for you, and an easy but exotic ravani that is pleasurable plain or with icing. My halvah—with fruit—has been served to great acclaim on two continents, and I go back to my roots in Crete with the Anoyiano kaltzouni, an heirloom recipe that works best with goat myzithra cheese and Greek thyme honey.

I start the section with a deeply licorice-flavored fig-ouzo sauce that will make Greek whatever you top with it, even ordinary vanilla ice cream.

Enjoy and *yassoo!*

Fig-Ouzo Sauce

The combination of figs with ouzo is as Greek as a fiery temperament and a desperate desire to enjoy every day to the hilt. This sauce for dairy—such as yogurt, ice cream, or fresh goat cheese—also works well as a stand-alone dessert. It is spectacular if made with fresh, ripe figs but works quite wonderfully with the infinitely more available (and affordable) dried figs.

1 cup boiling water
15 dried figs (preferably Greek),
   cut in half lengthwise
¼ cup granulated sugar
¼ cup ouzo
Chopped fresh mint, for garnish

Pour boiling water over dried figs and let stand for 10 minutes.

Transfer 3 of the soaked figs and all the soaking water to a blender and blend at high speed until saucy but somewhat gritty. (If using fresh figs, blend 3 of them with ½ cup cold water.)

Transfer blended figs to a saucepan. Stir in sugar. Cook, stirring, over medium-low heat for 3 to 4 minutes or until simmering. Add the rest of the figs and turn in the sauce for 4 to 5 minutes, until tender.

Raise heat to medium-high and add ouzo. Cook, stirring, for about 2 minutes, until alcohol evaporates. Transfer figs and juices to a bowl and let cool for about 20 minutes.

Serve figs on their own or as a topping for thick yogurt, ice cream, or cheese. Garnish with fresh mint.

Serves 4 or 5

Krema

Greek Custard

Sometimes the smallest detail will mark the success of a dessert. In this case it is the nutty masticha, a gum from a particular evergreen of the island of Chios. At one time a prized ingredient whose theft was considered a major crime, it is now available in North America, albeit at special Greek shops. It is marked "optional" because it can prove difficult to find, but seeking it out is worth the effort.

1½ cups whole milk
1 cup cream (35% or 18%)
1 cup granulated sugar
2 egg yolks, beaten
3 tbsp orange blossom water
1 tsp ground masticha (Greek evergreen gum)
   (optional)
1 tbsp cornstarch dissolved in 2 tbsp water
Ground cinnamon and rose-petal preserve,
   for garnish

In a saucepan, heat milk, cream, and sugar on medium heat, stirring, for about 5 minutes, until sugar is dissolved and mixture is hot but short of boiling. Reduce heat to medium-low and stir in egg yolks, orange blossom water, and optional masticha. Simmer, stirring constantly, for 2 minutes. Stir in cornstarch mixture and continue stirring for 1 to 2 minutes, until custard begins to thicken.

Transfer to custard bowls and let cool for 10 minutes. Cover and refrigerate until set.

Serve cold with a dusting of cinnamon and a spoonful of rose-petal preserve.

Serves 8

Rizogalo

Rice Pudding

Rice pudding is ubiquitous in Greek restaurants and homes, probably because it is so easy to make and such a universal palate pleaser. This one is dressed up with saffron, lemon zest, and rose-petal jam, which is more available than it sounds, usually imported from Bulgaria (the land of a billion roses).

6 cups whole milk
¾ cup granulated sugar
1 tsp saffron
1½ cups cooked rice
1 tbsp cornstarch dissolved in 2 tbsp water
¼ cup rose-petal jam
1 tsp grated lemon zest
1 tbsp lemon juice

In a saucepan, heat milk, sugar, and saffron over medium heat, stirring, for about 5 minutes, until sugar is dissolved and mixture is hot but short of boiling. Add cooked rice and cook, stirring, for 2 minutes. Stir in cornstarch mixture and continue stirring for 1 to 2 minutes, until pudding begins to thicken. Transfer to pudding bowls and let cool for 10 minutes. Cover and refrigerate until set.

Combine rose-petal jam, lemon zest, and lemon juice. Serve rice pudding cold with a dollop of the jam mixture.

Serves 8

Halvah with Fruit

A traditional dessert that every Greek enjoys from infancy onwards is here turned on its head with various complementary additions of spice, fruit, and nuts.

¾ cup mixed dried fruit of choice (such as sultana
   raisins, chopped apricots, chopped figs)
½ cup sweet white wine
¼ cup unsalted butter
1 cup coarse semolina
¾ cup granulated sugar
1 cup apple juice
1 cup water
1 tbsp grated orange zest
1 tbsp grated lemon zest
½ tsp grated nutmeg
½ tsp ground cardamom (optional)
¼ cup pine nuts
Glyko (preserve) of choice (quince is best;
   see page 172) and ground cinnamon, for garnish

Soak dried fruits in wine for at least 30 minutes.

Melt butter in large frying pan on medium heat for 1 minute. Add semolina and sugar; cook, stirring, for 3 minutes, until golden but not browned.

Add mixed fruits, apple juice, water, orange and lemon zests, nutmeg and optional cardamom. Stir until well mixed. Cook, stirring, for 3 to 4 minutes, until sticky and moist but still a little crunchy. Stir in nuts and remove from heat. Cover and let rest for 5 minutes.

Serve garnished with dollops of glyko and generous sprinkles of cinnamon.

Serves 4 to 6

Anoyiano Kaltsouni

Sweet Cheese Pie

Aristedes' native mountain village of Anoyia is famous for its clean air and its herb-fed sheep's milk, which is made into an array of cheeses, including myzithra, the fresh, unsalted curd that is often used in desserts. Here it is pan-browned in filo, and moistened by a boozy honey sauce. You could bake these instead in a 350°F oven for 10 to 12 minutes until golden, but I prefer the pan-drying method here. The pastry must be thin at the edges or it will not cook thoroughly.

12 oz fresh myzithra or ricotta cheese
¼ cup chopped fresh mint (or 1 tbsp dried)
1 tbsp granulated sugar
Pinch salt
½ cup honey (preferably thyme)
¼ cup Cretan raki or any eau-de-vie or vodka
2 sheets filo dough, cut in half lengthwise
2 to 3 tbsp melted unsalted butter or olive oil
Toasted white or black sesame seeds, for garnish

Combine cheese, mint, sugar, and salt in a bowl. Gently fold together just to mix. Set aside.

In a small saucepan, bring honey and raki just to the boiling point. Remove from heat and set aside.

Lay out half a sheet of filo on a dry surface with a short side facing you. Place about a quarter of the cheese mixture in the middle of the top third of the filo. Flatten mixture to a square, leaving a 1-inch margin at the top. Fold over the top flap and fold in the two side flaps. Using a pastry brush, lightly butter the flaps. Roll the stuffed part over the folds until you have formed a 2-inch by 4-inch envelope-shaped pie. Lightly brush butter on both sides of the pie. Repeat with the remaining filo and filling to make 4 pies.

Heat 2 large frying pans on medium heat for 3 minutes. Place 2 pies in each pan and cook for 3 to 4 minutes, until golden brown on the bottom. Turn and cook another 3 to 4 minutes, until golden brown. Transfer to plates, drizzle with honey syrup, sprinkle with sesame seeds, and serve immediately.

Serves 4

Ottoman Pumpkin

Sweetened pumpkin is at the heart of our most cherished holiday desserts. But, much as we love a rich pumpkin pie, this much leaner and more flavorful—not to mention historical—pumpkin delight offers just the right finishing note to already overloaded celebratory meals.

2 lb pumpkin, peeled, seeded, and cut
 into ½-inch-thick sticks
½ cup sweet white wine
 (such as samos or muscat)
¼ cup thyme or wildflower honey
2 tbsp sultana raisins
2 tbsp lemon juice
1 tsp grated nutmeg
½ tsp ground ginger
½ cup sour cream or vanilla ice cream
¼ cup walnut bits
Sprigs of fresh mint, for garnish

Heat large frying pan on high heat for 3 minutes. Add pumpkin and pan-dry, tossing, for 6 to 7 minutes, until slightly browned and just tender. Stir in wine, honey, raisins, lemon juice, nutmeg, and ginger. The juices will reach a bubble quickly. Cook, turning, coating the pumpkin in the sauce, for 2 to 3 minutes, until syrupy.

Spread portions of pumpkin on large plates and drizzle sauce around it. Dollop sour cream in the middle and sprinkle with walnuts. Stick a sprig of mint in the sour cream and serve immediately.

Serves 4

Apple Bougatsa

Greeks' love of filo dough does not just encompass spanakopita and baklava, it extends to all corners of gastronomy, even to these pudding-pies. It takes an Aristedes to make haute cuisine from such an inherently bland idea, and here you have his best effort. We think you'll agree that it works.

4 tbsp melted unsalted butter
¾ cup fine semolina
½ cup granulated sugar
1 tbsp grated orange and/or lemon zest
1 tsp vanilla seeds or extract
2 cups whole milk
¾ cup apple juice
8 sheets filo dough
1 cup thinly sliced apple
Icing sugar and ground cinnamon, for garnish

In deep pan over medium heat, heat 2 tbsp of the melted butter. Add semolina, sugar, orange zest, and vanilla. Cook, stirring, for 1 to 2 minutes, until butter is absorbed and semolina is golden but well short of browning. While whisking, add milk and apple juice in a steady stream, whisking until all the liquid is absorbed and there are no lumps. Cook, stirring, for 3 to 4 minutes, until mixture has the texture of runny cooked cream of wheat. Transfer to a bowl and let cool until firm.

Preheat oven to 350°F. Lay out a sheet of filo on a dry surface with a short end facing you. Place about an eighth of the semolina mixture in the middle of the top third of the filo, about 2 inches from the top edge, and spread it out to a flat square. Top semolina with one eighth of the apple slices. Fold over the top flap and fold in the two side flaps. Lightly brush flaps with some remaining melted butter. Roll the stuffed part over the folds until you have formed a 2-inch by 4-inch envelope-shaped pie. Lightly brush butter on both sides of the pie and transfer to a baking sheet. Repeat with remaining filo, filling, and apples to make 8 pies.

Bake pies for 8 to 10 minutes, until golden but not quite brown.

Serve immediately or let cool. Arrange 1 or 2 pies (according to appetite) on plates and dust with icing sugar and cinnamon (best done through a tea-strainer).

Serves 4 to 8

Greek Coffee-Cardamom Torte

This Greek variation of tiramisù offers a lovely bonus: its coffee-cardamom sauce can be used as a topping on other desserts, such as unfrosted cakes and plain ice cream.

Coffee-Cardamom Sauce
1½ cups water
⅔ cup granulated sugar
½ cup ground Greek coffee
1 tsp ground cardamom
1 tbsp cornstarch dissolved in 2 tbsp water
Cheese Filling
4 oz myzithra or ricotta cheese
½ cup icing sugar
2 tbsp 35% cream
Crumble
¼ cup unsalted butter
⅓ cup granulated sugar
⅓ cup all-purpose flour, sifted
1 tsp grated lemon zest

For coffee-cardamom sauce: Combine water, sugar, coffee, and cardamom in a saucepan and bring to simmer, stirring, on medium heat. Reduce heat to low and simmer, stirring, for 2 to 3 minutes (do not let boil). Remove from heat and let settle for 5 minutes.

Pass coffee mixture through a fine sieve and discard grounds. Return liquid to the saucepan and bring back to a simmer on medium heat. Stir in cornstarch mixture. Simmer, stirring, for 1 to 2 minutes, until somewhat thickened. Remove from heat and set aside to cool.

For cheese filling: In a bowl, beat myzithra, icing sugar, and cream until fluffy. Set aside.

For crumble: Heat small frying pan on medium-low heat for 3 minutes. Add butter and swirl until melted. Add sugar, sifted flour, and zest; cook, stirring, for 5 to 6 minutes, until butter is absorbed and crumble is brown. Remove from heat and let cool.

Press crumble into the bottom of a pie dish. Spread myzithra mixture over crumble. Refrigerate, covered, for at least 1 hour.

Serve cold with a generous topping of coffee-cardamom sauce.

Serves 6

Karithopita

Walnut Soufflé

A fluffy, nutty cake-soufflé that will have them begging for seconds is a splendid way to feature walnuts, the nut of choice of Greek desserts.

5 eggs, separated
1 tbsp melted unsalted butter
1 tbsp all-purpose flour
3 oz mascarpone cheese or
    softened unsalted butter
1 cup granulated sugar
1 cup ground walnuts
½ cup fine semolina
2 tbsp dark rum or Grand Marnier
1 tsp baking powder
Sour cream or ice cream (optional),
    for garnish

Beat egg whites until stiff but not dry. Cover and refrigerate.

Preheat oven to 325°F. Blend together butter and flour. Brush mixture on bottom and sides of a large soufflé dish.

In a mixing bowl, combine mascarpone and sugar, beating it into a paste. Add walnuts, semolina, rum, baking powder, and egg yolks. Beat until batter is well mixed and thick. Stir in one third of the beaten egg whites to lighten the batter, and fold in the rest gently but thoroughly, being careful not to deflate the whites.

Transfer batter to soufflé dish and bake for 45 minutes or until golden brown on top.

Serve immediately. For additional richness, garnish with optional sour cream or ice cream.

Serves 6

Ravani

Semolina Dessert

There are many versions of ravani, and all of them require a heavy dose of sugar syrup to drench it. Aristedes discovered that the cake is excellent without drenching, thus saving some calories, which he invests in a rich (and optional) topping. He includes a recipe for syrup, which is also optional. In either case, the amount of syrup used is minimal compared to what is traditional.

To make kumquat preserve, use the recipe for glyko (page 172), substituting kumquats cut in half lengthwise for the quince and omitting the citronella.

Syrup (optional)
1 tbsp lemon juice
1 cup granulated sugar
1 cup water
Cake
3 eggs, separated
¼ cup unsalted butter, softened
¾ cup granulated sugar

1 cup all-purpose flour
¾ cup coarse semolina
1 tsp baking powder
1 cup whole milk
2 tbsp grated orange and/or lemon zest
Topping (optional)
35% cream or ice cream (optional)
Fruit jam or preserve (kumquat is best) (optional)

For syrup: Combine syrup ingredients in a small saucepan. Bring to a boil, stirring, and boil gently until reduced by half and syrupy. Let cool.

For cake: Beat egg whites until stiff but not dry. Cover and refrigerate.

Preheat oven to 325°F. Lightly butter a 12-inch cake pan.

In a large bowl, beat butter and sugar into a smooth paste. Sift flour over butter mixture. Add semolina, baking powder, egg yolks, milk, and zest. Beat until batter is thick. Stir in one third of the beaten egg whites to lighten the batter, and fold in the rest gently but thoroughly, being careful not to deflate the whites.

Transfer batter to cake pan and bake for 30 minutes, until golden brown but still moist. If using syrup, puncture cake with a skewer all over and pour cooled syrup over hot cake. Let cool for about 1 hour, and serve on its own or with a generous dollop of cream or ice cream and a spoonful of your favorite jam or a scoop of preserved fruit.

Serves 8

Nutty Baklava

A staple of eastern Mediterranean cookbooks, restaurant menus, and countless pastry shops, baklava is simple to make, and so irresistible even when we are trying to cut down on calories. Aristedes, never content to leave well enough alone, offers three versions at once, and if you're feeling ambitious you could make some of each.

1 cup granulated sugar
1 cup water
2 tbsp orange blossom, lemon blossom,
   or rose water (optional)
2 tbsp lemon juice
4 sheets thin filo dough
½ cup melted unsalted butter

Walnut-Fig Filling
1½ cups walnut bits
¾ cup toasted fresh bread crumbs
½ cup dried figs cut in ½-inch pieces
1 tsp ground cinnamon

OR

Pistachio-Apricot Filling
1½ cups shelled natural pistachios
¾ cup toasted fresh bread crumbs
½ cup dried apricots cut in ½-inch pieces
½ tsp ground cardamom

OR

Almond-Chocolate Filling
1½ cups toasted slivered almonds
4 oz dark chocolate, finely chopped
¾ cup toasted fresh bread crumbs
½ cup candied orange rind cut in bits

Combine sugar and water and optional flavored water in a small saucepan on medium heat and bring to a boil, stirring occasionally. Stir in lemon juice. Boil for 6 to 7 minutes, until syrupy. Remove from heat and let cool. Set aside.

Place filling ingredients in blender and pulse several times until mixture is coarsely ground. Transfer to a bowl and stir in 2 tbsp cooled syrup. The mixture should loosely hold together but not be too wet and sticky.

Preheat oven to 350°F. Lightly butter a baking sheet. Lay out a sheet of filo on a dry surface. Using a pastry brush, lightly butter the filo. With a sharp knife or pizza cutter, cut filo lengthwise into 4 equal strips. Place strips of filo on flat surface brushed with a little melted butter.

Shape about 2 tbsp of the filling into a 3-inch-long cylinder. Place filling at one short end of a strip of filo. As tightly as possible, roll up filling inside filo to resemble a short cigar, with filling showing at each end. Place baklava on baking sheet. Repeat with remaining filo and filling to make 16 baklavas.

Lightly brush tops with butter. Bake for 8 to 10 minutes, until golden but not quite brown. Remove from oven and immediately spoon some syrup on each baklava. Let cool for a few minutes.

Serve 2 to 4 baklavas per person, according to appetite.

Makes 16 baklavas

Quince Glyko

Glyko is the most traditional of all Greek desserts (it simply means "sweet" in English), and most house-wives make their own favorite type, which they store in a jar to be taken out and served to special guests. Glyko is made from a range of vegetables, such as baby eggplant, tomatoes, carrots, or whole green nuts, as well as fruit, berries, and all varieties of citrus peel. This recipe can be used for all types of glyko.

Citronella leaves can be replaced by your favorite flavor: kefir lime leaves, lemon grass, marjoram, orange or lemon blossom water, rose water, and pomegranate juice are just a few of the flavors Aristedes has tried with excellent results.

5 cups water
2 cups granulated sugar
8 large citronella leaves
5 quince, peeled, cored, and cut into
    ¼-inch-thick wedges
3 tbsp lemon juice

In a large saucepan, bring water, sugar, and citronella leaves to a boil, stirring to dissolve sugar. Add quince and lemon juice; boil for 12 to 15 minutes, until liquid has reduced by about one quarter and is syrupy.

Remove from heat and continue stirring for 3 to 4 more minutes, until all the pieces of fruit are thoroughly coated and most of the syrup is clinging to the fruit.

To serve, simply place a tablespoon of glyko on a small plate, accompanied by a glass of ice water. Or serve with Ravani (page 170), ice cream, Krema (page 162), fresh soft cheese, or Kaimaki cream (similar to Devon cream).

Acknowledgments

I would like to thank my son, Orestes; his wife, Annelies Weiser; my sisters Agape and Chrisoula; my protégé, Harris Stamatopoulos, for his help in testing some of the recipes; and Alexia von Beck, whose help and encouragement was instrumental in this publication.

ARISTEDES PASPARAKIS

Index